DOIOFE

MANAGING TRANSITIONS

Other Books by William Bridges

Jobshift: How to Prosper in a Workplace without Jobs

Transitions: Making Sense of Life's Changes

Surviving Corporate Transition: Rational Management in a World of Mergers, Layoffs, Startups, Takeovers, Divestitures, Deregulation, and New Technologies

The Character of Organizations: Using Jungian Type in Organizational Development

A Year in the Life

MANAGING TRANSITIONS

Making the Most of Change

WILLIAM BRIDGES

PERSEUS BOOKS

Reading, Massachusetts

Perseus Books are available at special discounts for bulk purchases in the U.S. by corporations, institutions, and other organizations. For more information, please contact the Special Markets Department at HarperCollins Publishers, 10 East 53rd Street, New York, NY 10022, or call 212-207-7528.

Library of Congress Cataloging-in-Publication Data

Bridges, William, 1933–
    Managing transitions : making the most of change / William Bridges.
      p.   cm.
    Includes bibliographical references and index.
    ISBN 0-201-55073-3 (pbk. : alk. paper)
    1. Organizational change.   2. Industrial management. I. Title.
HD58.8.B75 1991
   658.4′06—dc20   91-573
                                                        CIP

Perseus Books is a member of the Perseus Books Group

Cover design by Richard Rossiter
Text design by Wilson Graphics and Design (Kenneth J. Wilson)
Set in 10-point Palatino by Shepard Poorman Communications Corp.

26 27 28 29—02010099

Find us on the World Wide Web at
http://www.aw.com/gb/

Contents

Acknowledgments

My approach to the management of organizational transition comes from 15 years of working with thousands of people in the transition seminars I have conducted. These were people who were going through career changes and divorces, who were moving and retiring, whose first child had just been born and whose last child had just left home—or, in some cases, had just returned home again after having apparently moved out for good. They were going through major changes in their health, financial situation, spiritual condition, or sexual orientation. They were coming of age, coping with midlife crises, and coming to terms with old age.

During the early 1980s, my work changed gradually but markedly. I redirected my attention to the organizational changes that were becoming more and more common: the mergers, reorganizations, layoffs, shifts in strategy or product or culture. I focused on the question of how managers could handle these organizational changes so that they did not leave the organization weaker instead of stronger. In the process I developed a new series of workshops that went under the title, "Managing Organizational Transition."

In 1991, these workshops have been conducted in several hundred organizations of all kinds: Fortune 500 corporations, fast-growing new companies and stable older ones, community and research hospitals, universities and community colleges, and federal, state and local agencies. In each case I conducted interviews to learn the problems associated with change and to find out what was working and what wasn't.

This book grows out of that work and represents my own best thinking about the subject at present. Some of it I discovered only a month ago, and some I worked out a decade ago. All of it I owe to the people in those companies who told me how change was affecting them and who shared what they had learned in the process.

There is no way to acknowledge all of them, but I want to thank a few who have been particularly helpful: Peg Sloan and Carol Tisson of Intel; Jim Schroth of Levi, Strauss; Debbie Biondolillo and Laurence Akiyoshi of Apple; Robert Levy, Kathleen Borges, and Patricia Moore of Hewlett-Packard; Frank Tuerlay of Pacific Bell; Ruth Welch of Adaptec; Frank Riddle of Stanford University; Nielson Buchanan, Cilla Raughley, and Dick Pettingill of El Camino Hospital; Andy Crouse of IBM; David Belsheim of Moore Business Systems;

Lorraine Zipirolli of Stanford Children's Hospital; Gary Merrill of Drake, Beam, and Morin; Gail Skinner of the Minnesota Extension Service; Larry Brunner of Procter & Gamble; Aaron Harris of ROLM; Charles deRidder of the U.S. Forest Service; and independent consultants Tom Ucko, Pat Newman, Bill Daniels, David Kyle, Marcia Palitz-Elliot, Ruth Morton, and Don Skilling. My credits would be longer if my memory was better.

I would also like to thank Curtis Brown, Ltd. and André Deutsch, Ltd. for permission to reprint from "Put Back Those Whiskers, I Know You," by Ogden Nash, Copyright © 1959 by Ogden Nash.

Special thanks go to Susan Schwartzbach and Marilyn Carosella, who make our business run; and to my colleague and daughter, Margaret Bridges, who has provided me with the support, assistance, criticism, and new ideas I have long needed. I want to thank my Addison-Wesley editor, Kate Habib, and production coordinator, Peggy McMahon, for getting the book through the terrible ordeal of publication with a minimum of pain. Finally, I thank my wife, Mondi, for being my partner and dear friend.

Introduction

He that will not apply new remedies must expect new evils.

— Francis Bacon, English philosopher

Faced with the choice between changing one's mind and proving that there is no need to do so, almost everybody gets busy on the proof.

— John Kenneth Galbraith, American economist

This book will help you to understand the difficulties you face whenever you try to get people to change the way they do things—the blank stares, muttering, foot-dragging, and subtle sabotage that turns a good plan into an unworkable mess. But it will give you more than understanding. It will also provide dozens of tactics—used by thousands of managers in other companies, nonprofits, government agencies, and universities—to help people cope with changes. These are specific tactics that you can use at your next team meeting.

The book is organized into four parts. The first gives you a new and useful perspective on the difficulties ahead and a test case to which you can apply your new knowledge. The second translates that understanding into practical actions you can take. The third gives you ways to deal with nonstop change, both organizationally and personally. The fourth provides another case on which to test your new tactics.

Often the changes you have to implement are important to the survival or success of your organization. They aren't the "it would be nice if we could do it" or the "do it if you get around to it" kind of change. They involve the different technology the organization needs to be competitive, the new structure it needs to be effective, the reduced level of overhead it needs to be profitable. Change is the game today, and organizations that can't deal with it effectively aren't likely to be around long.

All of this talk about helping people cope with change may strike you as unnecessary. You may see yourself as the kind of person who tells people what to do, and they do it. These days it would be truer to say that they *used to* do it. Simple, unquestioning compliance comes along less and less often.

For one thing, change happens so frequently today that one change isn't complete before another is being launched. Management guru Tom Peters tells us that we must "thrive on chaos," but very few workers show much interest in such a strenuous regimen. To make matters worse, in today's highly competitive marketplace, there's no margin for error. And when you mishandle a situation, employees may take legal action. For instance, employees are winning more than half of the wrongful discharge cases filed. Stress-related disability, including the claimed stress of working for you, is another increasingly common complaint.

You may be the kind of person who shies away from the difficulties of managing change because the people side of things isn't your strong suit. You're better at the functional tasks—getting out the product, delivering the service, providing the professional assistance—than you are at managing the human beings who do those things. You don't have the skills or the training to be a psychologist—you don't want to get into all that personal stuff. You just want to get results.

I sympathize. But a decade of working with people in your situation has convinced me of two things:

First, you simply cannot get the results you need without getting into "that personal stuff." The results, as we shall see in chapter 1, depend on getting people to stop doing things the old way and getting them to start doing things a new way. There is no way to do that impersonally.

Second, it doesn't take a degree in psychology to manage people in transition successfully. You're already using psychology—every time you try to guess a motive, figure out a tactful response in a difficult situation, or find a way to explain something effectively. Transition management takes some abilities you already have and some techniques you can easily learn. It isn't an undertaking that will offend anyone's sense of personal privacy, theirs or yours. Instead, it is a way of dealing with people that makes everyone feel more comfortable.

I respect your misgivings, but I think you'll find that they don't represent real obstacles. I'm not saying that transition management is easy—just that it is essential. If you don't know how to get started, this book is for you.

PART ONE

The Problem

Chapter 1

It Isn't the Changes That Do You In

Men believe that a society is disintegrating when it can no longer be pictured in familiar terms. Unhappy is a people that has run out of words to describe what is going on.

— Thurman Arnold, American lawyer

The beginning of wisdom is to call things by their right names.

— Chinese proverb

It isn't the changes that do you in, it's the transitions. Change is not the same as transition. *Change* is situational: the new site, the new boss, the new team roles, the new policy. *Transition* is the psychological process people go through to come to terms with the new situation. Change is external, transition is internal.

Here's an example. Varity Corporation, the Canadian agricultural equipment company that used to be called Massey-Fergusson, decided to change the information management system in its tractor division. Aaron Jones, director of finance and administration, noted that in the past they had always "retrieved information by country and not by how products were used, such as for narrow- or wide-row farming, vineyards, or orchards." So they changed. What happened? Jones discovered that the French employees had real affection for the French company, British employees for the U.K. company, and Italian employees for the Italian company. A lot of people saw their loyalty and interest connected much more closely to what happened to each of these companies than to the tractor division overall.[1] And so a useful change was undermined by the transitions that it caused in the employees who had to make it work.

Unless *transition* occurs, *change* will not work. That's what happens when a great idea falls flat. Not long ago a large insurance company ran a huge program in which 485 teams were set up to generate cost-saving ideas. The director of the effort later reported, with no apparent awareness of the irony of what he was saying, that "the most creative idea submitted to date and which supports the best intentions of the program, has potential annualized savings of $40,000. If paper inserted into a FAX machine is inserted sideways it will cut transmission time 15%." *He said, however, "that it will be hard to implement because it means changing behavior."* [2]

The change of clothes;
Changed, yes,
But the same lice of
my journeying.

Issa

At least he recognized that people have to reorient themselves psychologically if the situational difference is going to work. The old French saying puts the matter a little less positively: "The more things change, the more they stay the same." Translating that into the terms we are using, it means, "There can be any number of changes, but unless there are transitions, nothing will be different when the dust clears."

Several of the important differences between change and transition are overlooked when people think of transition as simply gradual or unfinished change. When we talk about change, we naturally focus on the outcome that the change will produce. If you move from California to New York City, the change is crossing the country and learning your way around the Big Apple. The same is true of your organization's change to a service culture or to a flatter organizational structure or to using electronic mail to communicate internally. In each case the new arrangements must be understood if we are to be ready for the change.

Transition is different. The starting point for transition is not the outcome *but the ending that you will have to make to leave the old situation behind.* Situational change hinges on the new thing, but psychological transition depends on letting go of the old reality and the old identity you had before the change took place. Nothing so undermines organizational change as the failure to think through who will have to let go of what when change occurs.

Transition starts with an ending—paradoxical but true. Test this fact in your own experience. Think of a big change in your life: your first managerial job, or the birth of your first child, or the move to a new house. Good changes, all of them, but as transitions, each one started with an ending.

With the job, you may have had to let go of your old peer group. They weren't peers anymore, and the kind of work you really liked may have come to an end. Perhaps you had to give up the feeling of competence that came from doing that work, and your habit of leaving your work at the office may have stopped when you took on the round-the-clock responsibility of a managerial job.

With the baby, you probably had to let go of regular sleep, extra money, time alone with your spouse, and the spontaneity of going somewhere when the two of you felt like it. Here, too, your sense of competence may have come to an end as you found yourself unable to get the baby to eat or sleep or stop crying.

With the move, a whole network of relationships ended. Even if you kept in touch, it was never the same again. You used to know where to go for what: stores, the doctor, the dentist, and the neighbor who'd keep an eye on the house when you were gone. You have to let go of feeling at home for a while.

Even in these "good" changes, there are transitions that begin with having to let go of something. There are endings. There are losses. I'm not trying to be discouraging—just realistic. The failure to identify and be ready for the endings and losses that change produces is the largest single problem that organizations in transition encounter.

The organization institutes a quality improvement program, and no one foresees how many people will experience the "improvement" as a loss of something related to their job. The organization builds a beautiful new headquarters building, and no one foresees how many people experience the relocation as a loss.

Once you understand that *transition begins with letting go of something,* you have taken the first step in the task of transition management. The second step is understanding what comes after the letting go: *the neutral zone.* This is the no-man's-land between the old reality and the new. It's the limbo between the old sense of identity and the new. It is a time when the old way is gone and the new doesn't feel comfortable yet.

When you moved to your new house, or got the promotion, or had the baby, the change probably happened pretty fast. But that is just the external situational change. Inwardly the psychological transition happened much more slowly, because instead of becoming a new person as fast as you changed outwardly, you actually struggled for a time in a state that was neither the old nor the new. It was a kind of emotional wilderness, a time when it wasn't clear who you were or what was real.

It's important to understand this neutral zone for several reasons. First, if you don't expect it and understand why it is there, you're likely to try to rush through it and to be discouraged when you cannot do so. You may mistakenly conclude that the confusion you feel is a sign that there's something wrong with you.

Second, you may be frightened in this no-man's-land and try to escape. (Employees do this frequently, which is why there is an increased level of

Every new truth which has ever been propounded has, for a time, caused mischief; it has produced discomfort and oftentimes unhappiness; sometimes disturbing social and religious arrangements, and sometimes merely by the disruption of old and cherished associations of thoughts. . . . And if the truth is very great as well as very new, the harm is serious.

Henry Thomas Buckle, English historian

turnover during major organizational changes.) To abandon the situation, however, is to abort the transition, both personally and organizationally—and to jeopardize the change.

Third, if you escape prematurely from the neutral zone, you'll not only compromise the change but also lose a great opportunity. Painful though it often is, the neutral zone is the individual's and the organization's best chance for creativity, renewal, and development. The positive aspect of the neutral zone will be discussed further in a later chapter, but here let me note simply that this gap between the old and the new is the time when innovation is most possible and when revitalization begins.

The neutral zone is thus both a dangerous and an opportune place, and it is the very core of the transition process. It's the place and time when the old habits that are no longer adaptive to the situation are extinguished and new, better-adapted patterns of habit begin to take shape. It is the winter in which the old growth returns to the soil as decayed matter, while the next year's growth begins to stir in the root underground. It is the night during which we are disengaged from yesterday's concerns and prepared for tomorrow's. It is the chaos in which the old form of things dissolves and from which the new form emerges. It is the seedbed of the new beginning that you seek.

It is a terrible thing to look over your shoulder when you are trying to lead—and find no one there.

Franklin Delano Roosevelt

Ending—neutral zone—new beginning. People make the new beginning only if they have first made an ending and spent some time in the neutral zone. Yet most organizations try to start with the beginning rather than finishing with it. They pay no attention to endings. They do not acknowledge the existence of the neutral zone, then wonder why people have so much difficulty with change.

When I say that "organizations" do these things, I mean, of course, that people do. Only people like you can develop the new attitude toward change by recognizing that it is dependent on transition. Only people like you can learn to manage transitions so the changes do not become unmanageable. Only people like you can implement change in such a way that it does not end up hurting the organization more than helping it.

The following pages will show you how to do those things.

---

[1] Quoted in Benjamin B. Tregoe, et al., *Vision in Action* (New York: Simon & Schuster, 1989).

[2] In "The Idea Generator," *HR Reporter*, V, 2 (February 1988), p. 3, italics added.

Chapter 2

A Test Case

We think in generalities, but we live in detail.

— Alfred North Whitehead, American philosopher

Chapter 1 was fairly theoretical. Unless you understand the basic transition model, you won't be able to use it. But only in actual situations can you use it, so let's look at a situation I recently encountered in a software company. I was brought in because the service manager wanted to make a change, and his staff was telling him it wasn't going to be as easy as he thought.

He told me that he didn't see why that should be so. The change made perfect sense, and it was also necessary for the firm's continued leadership in the field of business software for banks. "Besides," he said, "no one's going to lose a job or anything like that."

Bearing in mind what you read in chapter 1, see what you think.

The company's service unit did most of its business over the telephone. Individual technicians located in separate cubicles fielded callers' questions. The company culture was very individualistic. Not only were employees referred to as "individual contributors," but each was evaluated based on the number of calls he or she disposed of in a week. At the start of each year a career evaluation plan was put together for each employee in which a target (a little higher than the total of the previous year's weekly numbers) was set. To hit the target brought a bonus. To miss it cost one that bonus.

Purchasers of big, custom software packages called to report various kinds of operating difficulties, and the calls were handled by people in three different levels. First the calls went to relatively inexperienced individuals, who could answer basic questions. They took the calls on an availability basis. If the problem was too difficult for the first level, it went to the second echelon. Technicians at that level had more training and experience and could field most of the calls, but if they couldn't take care of a problem, they

7

passed it on to someone in echelon three. The "threes" were programmers who knew the system from the ground up and could, if necessary, tell the client how to reprogram the software to deal with the problem.

Each echelon was a skill-based unit with its own manager, who was responsible for managing the workload and evaluating the performance of the individual contributors. Not surprisingly, there was some rivalry and mistrust among the echelons, as each felt that its task was the pivotal one and that the others didn't pull their weight.

As you may have surmised, there were several inherent difficulties with this system. First, customers never got the same person twice unless they remembered to ask. Worse yet, there was poor coordination among the echelons. A level one technician never knew to whom he was referring a customer—or sometimes whether anyone at the next level actually took over the customers when he passed them on. Customers were often angry at being passed around rather than being helped.

Managers were very turf conscious, and this didn't improve coordination. Sometimes the second-echelon manager announced that all the "seconds" were busy—although this was hard to ascertain because each technician was hidden in a cubicle—and then the service would go on hold for a day (or even a week) while the seconds caught up with their workload. In the meantime, the frustrated customer might have called back and found that he had to start over again and explain the problem to a different first-echelon worker.

Customers were not only passed along from one part of the service unit to another, sometimes they were "mislaid" entirely. The level of customer satisfaction was mediocre at best. That hadn't been as damaging when the company had no real competition, but when another company launched an excellent new product earlier that year, it spelled trouble.

The general manager of the service unit brought in a service consultant, who studied the situation and recommended that the unit be reorganized into teams of people from each of the three echelons. (This is what in the last chapter I called the *change*.) A customer would be assigned to a team, and the team would have the collective responsibility of solving the customer's problem. Each team would have a coordinator responsible for steering the customer through the system of resources. Everyone agreed: the change ought to solve the problem.

The change was explained at a unitwide meeting, where large organization charts and team diagrams lined the walls. Policy manuals were rewritten, and the team coordinators—some of whom had been echelon managers and some of whom were former programmers—went through a two-day training seminar. The date for the cutover was announced, and each team met with the general manager, who told them how important the change was and how important their part was in making it work.

When the cutover occurred, there were problems. There are always problems with change, and so no one worried too much. But a month or so later it became clear that the new system not only wasn't working, it didn't even exist except on paper. The old echelons were still entrenched in everyone's mind, and customers were still being tossed back and forth (and often dropped) without any system of coordination. The coordinators maintained their old ties with people from their former echelons and tended to try to get things done with the help of their old people (even when those people belonged to another team) rather than by their team as a whole.

Imagine that you're brought in to help them straighten out this tangle. What would you do? Because we can't discuss the possibilities face to face, I will give you a list of actions that might be taken in such a situation. Scan them and see which sound like good ideas to you. Then go back through the list slowly and put a number by each item, assigning it one of the following five categories:

1 = Very important. Do this at once.

2 = Worth doing but takes more time. Start planning it.

3 = Yes and no. Depends on how it's done.

4 = Not very important. May even be a waste of effort.

5 = No! Don't do this.

Fill in those numbers before you read further, and take your time. This is not a simple situation, and solving it is a complicated undertaking.

_1_ Explain the changes again in a carefully written memo.

_2_ Figure out exactly how individuals' behavior and attitudes will have to change to make teams work.

_1_ Analyze who stands to lose something under the new system.

_5_ Redo the compensation system to reward compliance with the changes.

3   "Sell" the problem that is the reason for the change.

2   Bring in a motivational speaker to give employees a powerful talk about teamwork.

3   Design temporary systems to contain the confusion during the cutover from the old way to the new.

2   Use the interim between the old system and the new to improve the way in which services are delivered by the unit—and, where appropriate, create new services.

4   Change the spatial arrangements so that the cubicles are separated only by glass or low partitions.

5   Put team members in contact with disgruntled clients, either by phone or in person. Let them see the problem firsthand.

2   Appoint a "change manager" to be responsible for seeing that the changes go smoothly.

3   Give everyone a badge with a new "teamwork" logo on it.

5   Break the change into smaller stages. Combine the firsts and seconds, then add the thirds later. Change the managers into coordinators last.

2   Talk to individuals. Ask what kinds of problems they have with "teaming."

2   Change the spatial arrangements from individual cubicles to group spaces.

4   Pull the best people in the unit together as a model team to show everyone else how to do it.

3   Give everyone a training seminar on how to work as a team.

3   Reorganize the general manager's staff as a team and reconceive the GM's job as that of a coordinator.

2   Send team representatives to visit other organizations where service teams operate successfully.

4   Turn the whole thing over to the individual contributors as a group and ask them to come up with a plan to change over to teams.

5   Scrap the plan and find one that is less disruptive.

5   Tell them to stop dragging their feet or they'll face disciplinary action.

5   Give bonuses to the first team to process 100 client calls in the new way.

4   Give everyone a copy of the new organization chart.

1   Start holding regular team meetings.

1   Change the annual individual targets to team targets, and adjust bonuses to reward team performance.

2   Talk about transition and what it does to people. Give coordinators a seminar on how to manage people in transition.

There aren't any correct answers in this list, but over time I've come to trust some interventions more than others. Let me offer my lists in reverse order, *worsts* first. I'll make comments on each item.

Category 5: Don't do this!

Turn the whole thing over to the individual contributors as a group and ask them to come up with a plan to change over to teams.

Involvement is fine, but it has to be carefully prepared and framed within realistic constraints. Simply to turn the power over to people who don't want a change to happen is to invite catastrophe.

Break the change into smaller stages. Combine the firsts and seconds, then add the thirds later. Change the managers into coordinators last.

This one is tempting because small changes are easier to assimilate than big ones. But one change after another is trouble. It's better to introduce change in one coherent package.

Pull the best people in the unit together as a model team to show everyone else how to do it.

This is even more appealing, but it strips the best people out of the other units and hamstrings the other groups' ability to duplicate the model team's accomplishments.

Scrap the plan and find one that is less disruptive.

Forget this one! You had good reasons to make the change. It's your job to find out how to make it work.

Tell them to stop dragging their feet or they'll face disciplinary action.

Don't make threats. They build ill-will faster than they generate positive results. But do make expectations clear. People who don't live up to them will have to face the music.

Category 4: Not very valuable. Probably a waste of effort.

Explain the changes again in a carefully written memo.

When you put things in writing, people can't claim later that they weren't told. Memos are actually better ways of protecting the sender than they are of informing the receiver, however. And they are especially poor as ways to convey complex information—like how a reorganization is going to be undertaken.

Change the spatial arrangements so that the cubicles are separated only by glass or low partitions.

You're on the right track—individual cubicles *do* reinforce the old behavior—but this solution doesn't go far enough because it doesn't use space creatively to reinforce the new identity as "part of a team." See Category 2 for a better solution.

Give everyone a copy of the new organization chart.

An organization chart can help to clarify complex groupings and reporting relationships, but this solution is pretty straightforward. It's the new attitudes and behavior we're concerned with here, not which VP people report to.

Category 3: Yes and no. Depends on how it's done.

Bring in a motivational speaker to give employees a powerful talk about teamwork.

The problem is that by itself, this solution accomplishes nothing. And too often it *is* done by itself, as though, once "motivated," people would make the change they were supposed to. This method should be integrated into a comprehensive transition management plan to be effective.

Appoint a "change manager" to be responsible for seeing that the changes go smoothly.

This is a good idea if you have a well-planned undertaking, complete with communication, training, and support. But merely to appoint someone and say "make it happen" is unlikely to accomplish anything. If the person isn't very skilled, he or she may become simply an enforcer and weaken the change effort.

Give everyone a badge with a new "teamwork" logo on it.

Symbols are great, and you should use them, but most badges are meaningless bits of tinsel. They have to be part of a larger, comprehensive effort. (A lot of issues come back to that point, and so will we.)

Give everyone a training seminar on how to work as a team.

Seminars are important because people have to learn the new way. But much training is wasted because it's not part of a larger, comprehensive effort.

Give bonuses to the first team to process 100 client calls in the new way.

Rewards and competition can both serve your effort, but be sure not to set simplistic quantitative goals. Those 100 clients can be "processed" in ways that send them right into the competition's arms. In addition, speed can be achieved by a few team members doing all the work. You want to reward *teamwork,* so plan your competition carefully.

Category 2: Worth doing but takes more time. Start planning it.

Redo the compensation system to reward compliance with the changes.

This is important because you need to stop rewarding the old behavior. But do it carefully. A reward system that comes off the top of someone's head is likely to introduce new problems faster than it clears up old ones.

Design temporary systems to contain the confusion during the cutover from the old way to the new.

The time between the end of old ways and the beginning of new ones is a dangerous period. Things fall through the cracks. More about this will be covered when we talk about the neutral zone, but for now suffice to say that you may have to create temporary policies, procedures, reporting relationships, roles, and even technologies to get you through this chaotic time.

Use the interim between the old system and the new to improve the ways in which services are delivered by the unit—and, where appropriate, create new services.

This is the flip side of the "in-between time": when things are up for grabs and innovations can be introduced more easily than during stable times. It's a time to try doing things in new ways—especially new ways people have long wanted to try but which conflicted with the old ways.

Change the spatial arrangements from individual cubicles to group spaces.

Until this is done, the new human configuration has no connection with the physical reality of the place. Space is symbolic. If they're all together physically, people are more likely to feel together mentally and emotionally.

Reorganize the general manager's staff as a team and reconceive the GM's job as that of a coordinator.

Leaders send many more messages than they realize or intend to. Unless the leader is modeling the behavior that he or she is seeking to develop in others, things aren't likely to change very much. As Ralph Waldo Emerson said, "What you are speaks so loudly I can't hear what you say."

Send team representatives to visit other organizations where service teams operate successfully.

People need to see, hear, and touch to learn effectively. Talking to someone who's actually doing something carries more weight with a doubtful person than even the best seminar or the most impressive pep talk. If you can't take people to another location, invite a representative to your location and ask for a videotape.

Change the annual individual targets to team targets, and adjust bonuses to reward team performance.

It's hard to get people who are used to going it alone to play on a team, and you'll never succeed until the game is redefined as a team sport. Annual performance schedules are part of what defines the game. Make this important change as soon as you can.

Category 1: Very important. Do this at once.

Figure out exactly how individuals' behavior and attitudes will have to change to make teams work.

To deal successfully with *transition*, you need to determine precisely what changes in their existing behavior and attitudes people will have to make. It isn't enough that they have to work as a team. They need to know how teamwork differs behaviorally and attitudinally from the way they are working now. What must they stop doing and what are they going to have to start doing? Be specific. Until these changes are spelled out, people won't be able to understand what you tell them.

Analyze who stands to lose something under the new system.

This step follows the previous one. Remember, transition starts with an ending. You can't grasp the new thing until you've let go of the old thing. It's this process of letting go that people resist, not the change itself. Their resistance can take the form of foot-dragging or sabotage, and you have to understand the pattern of loss to be ready to deal with the resistance and keep it from getting out of hand.

"Sell" the problem that is the reason for the change.

Most managers and leaders put 10% of their energy into selling the problem and 90% into selling the solution to the problem. People aren't in the market for solutions to problems they don't see, acknowledge, and understand. They might even come up with a better solution than yours, and then you won't have to sell it—it will be theirs.

Put team members in contact with disgruntled clients, either by phone or in person. Let them see the problem firsthand.

This is part of selling the problem. As long as you are the only one fielding complaints, poor service is going to be *your* problem, no matter how much you try to get your subordinates to acknowledge its importance. To engage their energies, you must make poor service *their* problem. Client visits are the best opportunity for people to see how their operation is perceived by its customers. DuPont has used this program very successfully in a number of its plants. Under its "Adopt a Customer" program, blue-collar workers are sent to visit customers once a month and to bring what they have learned back to the factory floor.

Talk to individuals. Ask what kinds of problems they have with "teaming."

When an organization is having trouble with change, managers usually say they know what is wrong. But the truth is that often they don't. They imagine that everyone sees things as they do, or they make assumptions about others which are untrue. You need to ask the right questions. If you ask, "Why aren't you doing this?" you've set up an adversarial relation and will probably get a defensive answer. If, on the other hand, you ask, "What problems are you having with this?" you're likelier to learn why it isn't happening.

Talk about transition and what it does to people. Give coordinators a seminar on how to manage people in transition.

Everyone can benefit from understanding transition. A coordinator will deal with subordinates better if he or she understands what they are going through. If they understand what transition feels like, team members will feel more confident that they haven't taken a wrong turn. Never pretend that change is easy. Everyone can deal with transition better if they understand what is hard about it and what can be done about it.

Start holding regular team meetings.

Even before you can change the space to fit the new teams, you can start building the new identity by having those groups meet regularly. In the organization referred to earlier, the plan had been to hold meetings every two weeks. We changed that immediately: The teams met every morning for ten minutes for the first two months. Only such frequent clustering can override the old habits and the old self-images and build the new relations that teamwork requires. And you can give no stronger message about a new priority than to give it a visible place on everyone's calendar.

In the foregoing example of how a situation might be handled, it's important that your answers dealt successfully with *transition* and that you chose tactics that would not merely change the situation but would help people make the psychological reorientation that must happen if change is to work. The following chapters will provide dozens of tactics that have proved helpful in managing transition.

In chapter 8 you'll find another case and another chance to try your hand at a transition management plan. But first let's look at some well-tested transition management tactics. Chapters 3, 4, and 5 will deal, respectively, with how to manage endings, neutral zones, and new beginnings. Chapter 6 deals with managing nonstop change, and chapter 7 provides ways to manage your own situation better. When you reach the next case study, you'll be full of ideas.

PART TWO

The Solutions

Chapter 3

How to Get Them to Let Go

Every beginning is a consequence. Every beginning ends something.

— Paul Valery, French poet

Almost anything is easier to get into than out of.

— Agnes Allen, American epigrammatist

Before you can begin something new, you have to end what used to be. Before you can become a different kind of person, you must let go of the old identity. Before you can learn a new way of doing things, you have to unlearn the old way. So beginnings depend on endings. The problem is, people don't like endings.

Yet change and endings go hand in hand: Change causes transition, and transition starts with an ending. If things change, at least some employees and managers are going to have to let go of something. Here are some examples:

1. A hospital administrator decides to consolidate maternal and pediatric services. She recognizes that the reorganization makes terrific sense from the patient's point of view, and it will save overhead costs as well. But right now there are two completely different organizations, two different patterns of loyalty, two different sets of career paths, two different sets of procedures. There are even two organizational "characters," one developed from working with adults and one developed from working with children. Each of these differences is a part of unit members' separate identities. Each one talks about "us" and "them." People will have to let go of a whole world to make the new arrangement work.

2. The newly appointed controller of a large corporation decides to reorganize the archaic and inefficient way in which financial transactions are handled. The old work flow was a "bucket brigade," where the whole line

worked only as fast as its slowest bucket-handler and an embarrassingly large amount of business got "spilled" along the way. So he redesigns the work flow, and to make the new process work, he redesigns the organizational chart. Formerly separate functions are combined, and formerly joined functions are separated. People have new bosses, and the bosses have new responsibilities. Managers depend on the cooperation of people they don't know well, and they miss their buddies who used to help them get the job done in the old way.

3. A new general manager arrives at a manufacturing plant and finds that there are eight layers of supervision and management between him and the hourly workers. Information takes forever to move up or down the line, and when it arrives, it is often distorted. Decisions take months as problems are bumped up a level at a time, until finally someone acts. Then implementation takes forever as it filters down level by level. "Too many managers," he announces. "We're going to trim the work force and flatten the pyramid." Of the 60 managers and supervisors, 17 are close to retirement anyway, so they are lured out the door with sweetened retirement benefits. Six others are simply laid off, and 10 more are "reassigned"— which means "demoted," but no one will admit that. "There," says the GM. "Now we're trim and efficient." But as months go by, the results get worse and worse. People are dragging their feet. Rumors abound. The GM keeps talking about how much better the new structure is than the old, hoping that somehow he can convince people to make it work. In logical terms it is better, but he doesn't realize that it means little to people who have lost their familiar turf, their sense of self-worth, and many of their good friends.

It isn't the *changes* themselves that the people in these cases resist. It's the losses and endings that they experience and the *transition* that they are resisting. That's why it does little good to talk about how healthy the outcome of the change will be. Instead, you have to deal directly with the losses and endings.

But how do you do that? Here's how.

Identify Who's Losing What

What is actually ending and who is, in fact, losing what? If you're in the planning stage, this can be done in the following sequence.

1. Describe the change in as much detail as you can. *What is actually going to change?* Be specific. Terms like "improved quality," "decentralized decision making," and "lower costs" don't tell people specifically what is going to be different when the dust clears.

2. Imagine that the change is a cue ball rolling across the surface of a pool table. There are lots of other balls on the table, and it's going to hit a few of them, some because you planned it that way and some unintentionally. Try to foresee as many of those hits as you can. *What are the secondary changes that your change will probably cause? And what are the further changes that those secondary changes will cause?* As before, with each of those changes, describe exactly what will be different when the change is completed.

3. You have now started a chain of cause-and-effect collisions. For each of them, think of the people whose familiar way of being and doing will be affected. In each case, *who is going to have to let go of something?* What must they let go of: their peer group, the roles that gave them a sense of competence, their chances for promotion, the strategies that fit with their values, or their old expectations?

4. Beyond these specific losses, ask *what is over for everyone?* Is it a chapter in the organization's history? Is it an unspoken assumption about what the employees can expect from their employer? Is it something that the organization stands for? Whatever has ended might be summarized in a phrase like these:

   > We take care of our people.
   >
   > We are a cutting-edge, high-tech company.
   >
   > We won't settle for finishing second.
   >
   > We won't be undersold.
   >
   > We will always act ethically.
   >
   > We promote from within.

If, on the other hand, the change is already under way, you can find out about losses much more quickly. Simply ask people. "What's different now that we have a new X?" "When we did X, what did you have to give up?" "What do you miss since we changed X?"

Accept the Reality and Importance of the Subjective Losses

Don't argue with what you hear. In the first place, it will stop the conversation and you won't learn any more. In the second place, loss is a subjective experience, and your "objective" view (which is really just another subjective view) is irrelevant. Finally, you'll just make your task more difficult by convincing people that you don't understand them—or, worse yet, that you don't care what they feel and think.

We have come out of the time when obedience, the acceptance of discipline, intelligent courage and resolution were most important, into that more difficult time when it is a person's duty to understand the world rather than simply fight for it.

Ernest Hemingway, American writer

Maybe you don't care. Maybe in the old days when you learned how to manage people, you learned to give orders and to crack the whip if they weren't carried out. Compliance was enough in those days because there wasn't much competition and it took only half of people's energy and intelligence to do a decent job. Today it's different. Compliance isn't enough. You need everyone's commitment because only with commitment will you get people to give 100%. And you won't get people's commitment unless you understand them and make decisions based on that understanding. So however you do it, learn who is experiencing a loss of some kind and what it is they are losing.

Don't Be Surprised at "Overreaction"

People "overreact" to a change when they are reacting more than we are. But when we think that way, we overlook two things: first, that changes cause transitions, which cause losses—and it is the losses, not the changes, that they're reacting to; and second, that it's a piece of *their* world that is being lost, not ours—and that we often react that way when it's part of ourselves that is being lost. Being reasonable is much easier if one has little or nothing at stake.

Overreaction also comes from how past losses have been experienced. When old losses haven't been adequately dealt with, a sort of *transition deficit* is created—a readiness to grieve that only needs an ending to set it off. We see this when people overreact to the dismissal of an obviously ineffective manager or leader, or to some apparently insignificant change in policy or procedure. What they are actually reacting to is one or more losses in the past that have occurred without any acknowledgment or chance to grieve.

This same kind of overreaction occurs when an ending is viewed as symbolic of some larger loss. The minor layoff in a company that has never had layoffs before is an example. It isn't the loss of the particular individuals—it's the loss of the safety people felt from the no-layoff policy.

Overreactions also take place when a small loss is perceived as the first step in a process that might end with removing the grievers themselves. Someone whose job seemed secure is dismissed, and a hundred coworkers begin to wonder, "Am I next?"

In all of these cases overreaction is normal and not really overreaction at all. Learn to look for the loss behind the loss and deal with that underlying issue. You'll get much further if you can show people that Loss A is really unrelated to the dreaded, larger Loss B than if you simply try to talk them out of their reaction to Loss A.

Acknowledge the Losses Openly and Sympathetically

You need to bring losses out into the open—acknowledge them and express your concern for the affected people. Do it simply and directly:

> "I'm sorry that we're having to make these transfers. We're losing good people."

> "I know that switching to the new software is going to leave a lot of you feeling like beginners again. I feel that way myself, and I hate it!"

> "Hey, Charlie, I heard that you got the pink slip. That's really tough! I wish they could have figured some way around that."

Managers are sometimes loathe to talk so openly, even arguing that it will "stir up trouble" to acknowledge people's feelings. What such an argument misses is that it is not talking about a loss but, rather, pretending that it doesn't exist that stirs up trouble.

An electronics company recently had to lay off several dozen longtime employees, and fairly attractive severance packages were put together to reward them for their loyal service. It happened that these workers had to stay on for two months after the announcement was made, and their manager explained that he wasn't going to talk to them explicitly about their loss "because calling attention to it will just make them feel worse." His silence made them feel so angry that several of them began plotting ways to sabotage his unit's key project.

What that manager was really saying was that he didn't know how to handle the pain his employees felt. Many people find it difficult to deal openly with others' pain. But a great deal of research about what helps

I know that most men, including those at ease with problems of the greatest complexity, can seldom accept even the simplest and most obvious truth if it be such as would oblige them to admit the falsity of conclusions which they have delighted in explaining to colleagues, which they have proudly taught to others, and which they have woven, thread by thread, into the fabric of their lives.

Leo Tolstoy, Russian writer

people recover from loss suggests that they recover more quickly if the losses can be openly discussed.

I saw this point demonstrated recently in a factory that had been targeted for closure. I watched a crowd of upset employees listening to an executive explain why their plant was being scheduled for closure relax and drop their belligerent manner when the executive interrupted his explanation to express his personal distress at having to close the plant. The man later apologized to several of us for the "display of emotion," not realizing that his honest feeling won the employees over more than his logical explanation.

Expect and Accept the Signs of Grieving

When endings take place, people get angry, sad, frightened, depressed, confused. These emotional states can be mistaken for bad morale, but they aren't. They are the *signs of grieving*, the natural sequence of emotions people go through when they lose something that matters to them. You find them among families that have lost a member, and you find them in an organization where an ending has taken place.

Yet those emotions may not be evident, especially at first. People may deny that the loss will take place. *Denial* is a natural first stage in the grieving process, a way in which hurt people protect themselves from the first impact of loss. It is healthy and doesn't demand action on your part if it doesn't last very long. But if your people stay in denial for more than a few days after the handwriting is legible on the wall, you're going to need to address the issue. You may want to say something like this: "A lot of you are acting as though X isn't for real. Well, it is. Your actions concern me because I want all of us to get through this change with as little distress and disruption as possible. We'll never do that if we pretend it isn't happening."

Many a man would rather you heard his story than granted his request.

Phillip Stanhope, Earl of Chesterfield

As for the rest of the emotions grieving people feel, treat them seriously, but don't consider them as something you personally caused. Don't get defensive or argue. Here are some of those emotions and what you can do to deal with them successfully.

> *Anger: Everything from grumbling to rage, often misdirected or undirected. Can lead to foot-dragging, "mistakes," and even sabotage.* Listen . . . acknowledge that the anger is understandable. Don't take on the blame if it is being misdirected toward you. Distinguish between the acceptable

feelings and unacceptable acting-out behavior: "I understand how you feel, but I'm not going to let you mess up the project."

Bargaining: Unrealistic attempts to get out of the situation or to make it go away; trying to strike a special deal; making big promises that they'll "save you a bundle of money" or "double the output" if you'll only undo the change. Distinguish these efforts from real problem solving; keep a realistic outlook and don't be swayed by desperate arguments and impossible promises.

Anxiety: Silent or expressed; a realistic fear of an unknown and probably difficult future, or simply catastrophic fantasies. Anxiety is natural, so don't make people feel stupid for feeling it. Just keep feeding them the information as it comes, and commiserate with them when it doesn't.

Sadness: Everything from silence to tears—the heart of the grieving process. Encourage people to say what they are feeling, and share your feelings too. Don't try to reassure people with unrealistic suggestions of hope. Sympathize.

Disorientation: Confusion and forgetfulness even among organized people; feelings of being lost and insecure. Give people extra support—opportunities to get things off their chests, reassurances that disorientation is natural and that other people feel it too. And give them extra attention.

Depression: Feelings of being down, flat, dead; feelings of hopelessness and being tired all the time. Like sadness and anger, depression is hard to be around. You can't make it go away, however. People have to go through it, not around it. Make it clear that you understand and even share the feeling yourself, but that work still needs to be done. Do whatever you can to restore people's sense of having some control over their situations.

Not everyone feels all of these feelings intensely, and people don't go through them by the numbers. But in any group you can expect to encounter all of them, and you need to get people to recognize that they can accept the situation and move forward if they can work through these emotions. If you suppress the feelings and push people to get over them, you'll be handicapped with people who never "mended." In my work I see teams, departments, and

He that lacks time to mourn, lacks time to mend.

William Shakespeare, English dramatist

sometimes entire companies fall apart because they never found a way to grieve over a significant loss.

Compensate for the Losses

Many change efforts fail because the people affected feel only the pain. The company may gain, but for employees it seems to be all loss. Trying to talk them out of their feelings will get you nowhere. Find a way to act. Here are some examples:

1. A large financial services company reorganized its clerical force and retrained the clerks to do what the lead clerks and the supervisors had formerly done. These latter folks were going to be merely clerks under the new system, and they did everything they could to badmouth and undermine the new plans. Then the manager had an idea. She brought them together as a "training task force" to create a program—not only to bring their former subordinates up to speed but also to train new hires. Although these "demoted" people lost hierarchical status, they were given new status as technical experts and trainers, and they kept the new roles even after the change was accomplished. Their opposition turned slowly into cooperation and support.

2. The U.S. Forest Service went through funding cutbacks in the early 1980s. As the logging industry declined, so did the need for the timber specialists who had been the backbone of the service. At the same time, recreation gained more prominence, as did ecology, public information, computer services, and wildlife biology. The old-line foresters lost promotions, power, even jobs. So, following the principle of giving back in one area what had been lost in another, the Forest Service instituted career renewal programs to help people reorient their careers to the areas where opportunity was increasing. They even helped people plan new careers outside the Forest Service. People still felt their losses, but they moved through the grieving process and quickly became productive again.

3. A large state university reassigned one of its vice presidents to a far less important area than the one he had previously headed. Everyone knew that he had been ineffective in his previous job, so although no one called it a demotion, it was hard to see it as anything else. The new job actually fit his talents far better, but he was deeply hurt by the move. Discussing the situation, we discovered that the man was far less troubled by the fact of

the move than by how it would be perceived by his colleagues. Understanding the VP's real interests, the president was able to negotiate how the announcement would be made and how the move would be explained. A crippling loss was turned into a temporary hurt, and a solid (if overpromoted) employee was saved.

The question to ask yourself is, *what can I give back to balance what's been taken away?* Is it status, turf, team membership, or recognition? If people feel that the change has robbed them of control over their futures, can I find some way to give them back a feeling of control? If the feeling of competence has been taken away when their job disappeared, can I give them new feelings of competence in other functions with timely training?

> *Every exit is an entry somewhere else.*
>
> Tom Stoppard, American dramatist

  This principle of compensating for losses is basic to all kinds of change, and even the most important or beneficial changes often fail because this principle is overlooked. As journalist Walter Lippmann said 50 years ago: "Unless the reformer can invent something which substitutes attractive virtues for attractive vices, he will fail." Remember Lippmann's advice when you try to get people to accept programs in quality improvement or customer service, when you try to set up self-managed teams or introduce unfamiliar equipment, or when you flatten the organization or cut overhead.

Give People Information, and Do It Again and Again

There are lots of rationalizations for not communicating. Here are some common ones:

1. *They don't need to know yet. We'll tell them when the time comes. It'll just upset them now.* For every week of upset that you avoid by hiding the truth, you gain a month of bitterness and mistrust. Besides, the grapevine already has the news, so don't imagine that your information is a secret.

2. *They already know. We announced it.* OK, you told them, but it didn't sink in. Threatening information is absorbed remarkably slowly. Say it again. And find different ways to say it and different media (large meetings, one-on-ones, memos, a story in the company paper) to say it.

3. *I told the supervisors. It's their job to tell the rank and file.* The supervisors are likely to be in transition themselves, and they may not even sufficiently understand the information to convey it accurately. Maybe they're

still in denial. Information is power, so they may not want to share it yet. Don't assume that information trickles down through the organizational strata reliably or in a timely fashion.

4. *We don't know the details ourselves, so there's no point in saying anything until everything has been decided.* In the meantime, people can get more and more frightened and resentful. Much better to say what you do know, say that you don't know more, and tell what kind of schedule exists for additional information. If information isn't available later when it was promised, don't forget to say something to show that you haven't forgotten your promise.

Of course, there may be times when information must be withheld temporarily. The Securities and Exchange Commission may require it, for example, or you may not be able to talk about a strategic move because competitors will learn of it. But most of the time information is withheld because leaders or managers are afraid to give it. That fear often arises not from the anticipated long-term effects but simply from the short-term impact—the setting off of emotions discussed earlier under the heading of "grieving."

So instead of telling the truth, managers substitute a fabrication of half-truths and outright untruths. Not only do these later turn out to be outright lies, but managers often trip themselves up with inconsistencies and new stories to cover the old inconsistencies.

Those who honestly mean to be true contradict themselves more rarely than those who try to be consistent.

Oliver Wendell Holmes, Jr.,
American jurist

Define What's Over and What Isn't

One of the biggest problems that endings cause in an organization is confusion. Things change, and obviously we won't do some of the things we used to do. But which things? The boss says, "From here on, we're lean and mean!" Does that mean that we must order 30% fewer supplies, or that we don't sweat the little stuff any more, or that we have to give up the prospect of 40-hour weeks? The boss says, "We're really going to be customer-minded from now on." Do we do everything the customer says? What about company policy and standard procedures—are they out the window? The boss says, "We're increasing spans of control by 50%." Does that mean that managers do all the old stuff faster or that they can let go of some of the old stuff?

Not specifying what is over and what isn't runs the risk of three equally serious difficulties:

1. People won't dare to stop doing anything. They'll try to do all the old things *and* the new things. After a while they'll burn out with the overload.

2. People will make their own decisions about what to discard and what to keep, and the result will be chaos.

3. People will toss out everything that was done in the past, and the baby will disappear with the bathwater.

So think through each aspect of the change you are implementing, and be specific about what goes and what stays. It takes time to do that, but undoing the damage wrought by the three problems listed above will take much longer.

Mark the Endings

Don't just talk about the endings—create actions or activities that dramatize them. When René McPherson took over the leadership of Dana Corporation, he found operations choked by a culture in which everything was covered by rules, which, though incredibly detailed, nonetheless failed to cover all cases. Besides, no one could remember them all or even be sure in which of the company manuals a given rule could be found. He wanted to change to a culture in which there were a few universally understood principles and in which the employees' intelligence and commitment were counted on to apply the principles wisely.

He explained all this, but when it came time to make the change, he chose action rather than words to convey his point. In a management meeting he piled all the company manuals on a table. They formed a stack almost two feet tall. Then he swept them onto the floor and held up a single sheet of paper on which the corporate principles were typed. "These are our new rules," he said.

If you want an even more dramatic action, think of the Spanish conquistador, Cortés. When he came ashore with his men at Veracruz, he knew that they had great ambivalence about the task ahead of them. Some called it hopeless. Faced with a continent full of adversaries, everyone must have wished that he had never come. Cortés burned the ships.

A bit heavy-handed, perhaps. Think back to the Software Service Division example I described in chapter 2. In changing from individual contributors to teams, they tore down the walls of the service technicians' cubicles and created work team spaces in which people could see and talk to their new collaborators. On a functional level the new space worked better. But just as important, the act of creating it sent a message: "The old way of separation is gone. We're doing things a new collaborative way now."

Treat the Past with Respect

Never denigrate the past. Many managers, in their enthusiasm for a future that is going to be better than the past, ridicule or talk slightingly of the old way of doing things. In doing so they consolidate the resistance against the transition because people identify with the way things used to be and thus feel that their self-worth is at stake when the past is attacked.

But managers who are tempted to denounce the past are not all wrong: they are right in wanting to distinguish what they are proposing from what has been tried in the past or what is being done in the present. The trick is to make the distinction nonjudgmentally. Here are some examples:

An executive is brought in to reorganize a division into business units. Rather than attacking the old functional organization as inefficient and archaic ("Nobody in his right mind would run a business *that* way!"), he credits it for bringing the organization to the point where it now stands: on the brink of an important development. He emphasizes the continuities he feels with his predecessor and talks about the new challenges that call for new responses.

Historic continuity with the past is not a duty, it is only a necessity.

Oliver Wendell Holmes, American physician

The new director of a human resources department realizes that the compartmentalism of her group in the past has meant that conflicting policies developed and turf battles made cooperation impossible. She avoids the devastating critique that she could deliver and instead sends key personnel out to visit customers—who deliver her critique for her. She then exposes key members of the old order to a couple of organizations where teamwork has greatly improved service and helps them formulate and spearhead plans for the change.

Be careful that in urging people to turn away from the past, you don't drive them away from you or from the new direction that the organization needs to take. Present innovations as developments that build on the past and help to realize its potential. Honor the past for what it has accomplished.

Let People Take a Piece of the Old Way with Them

Endings occur more easily if people can take a bit of the past with them. You are trying to disengage people from it, not stamp it out like an infection. And in particular, you don't want to make people feel blamed for having been part of it.

When Western Airlines was sold to Delta, the Employee Store at Los Angeles International Airport sold out of all items with the big red "W" company logo in a few hours. When the Almaden Winery was sold to developers, employees lost one of the loveliest workplaces one could imagine. They grieved especially for the winery rose garden, where people had strolled during breaks and spent lunch hours. Management discovered that the employees were going into the garden after work and taking rose cuttings to take home. Recognizing the significance of what was happening, management decided to help by providing the cuttings themselves.

Organizations can take even more initiative in tapping this longing for a piece of the past. A Procter & Gamble paper plant in northern Michigan put together a yearbook during the last year of the plant's operation. People brought in pictures, some twenty or thirty years old, and wrote little essays about the past. The "graduating class" of current workers was featured, along with such information as was available about where everyone was going after "graduation."

Show How Endings Ensure Continuity of What Really Matters

Most endings are not so terminal as a plant closure or the sale of a company. In fact, many endings represent the only way to protect the continuity of something bigger. An out-of-date product line is discontinued and replaced so that a manufacturing company can keep its customers. Two hospitals merge (and lose their individual identities) because neither will be able to survive alone. The start-up company's seat-of-the-pants operating style, though exciting, is not adequate to manage the midsized company it has grown into. The old ways have to be relinquished before new systems will work. Again, people have to let go of a piece of their identity to protect the integrity of the whole.

A corollary to this idea is that the past, which people are likely to idealize during an ending, was itself a time of change. When people start talking about "the good old days," it's easy to imagine that they are describing a

A state without the means of some change is without the means of its conservation.

Edmund Burke, British statesman

Only the provisional endures.

French proverb

peaceful time of stability. But that is selective memory. There were changes then, too. Whenever something that is viewed as a controversial and dangerous break with the past turns out successfully, people forget the loss they felt when the change happened and begin to celebrate it as a tradition.

Yesterday's ending launched today's success, and today will have to end if tomorrow's changes are to take place. That doesn't make endings comfortable for any of us, but it does mean that they're not an unprecedented break with the past either. And it doesn't mean that they are simply an attempt by those in power to make people's lives miserable.

Conservatism is the worship of dead revolutions.

Clinton Rossiter, American historian

A Final Thought

In taking possession of a state, the conqueror should well reflect as to the harsh measures that may be necessary, and then execute them at a single blow. . . . Cruelties should be committed all at once.

Niccolo Machiavelli, Italian political philosopher

With all of the foregoing emphasis on foreseeing and softening the painful effects of loss on employees, the reader might assume that I am urging slowly taking things away a piece at a time. That would be a misreading of my advice, for the last thing an organization needs is too small an ending or an incomplete ending that requires a whole new round of losses to finish the job before the wounds from the old ones have healed. Whatever must end, *must end.* Don't drag it out. Plan it carefully, and once it is done, let there be time for healing. But the action itself should be sufficiently large to get the job done.

Conclusion

It doesn't work to leap a twenty-foot chasm in two ten-foot jumps.

American proverb

The single biggest reason organizational changes fail is that no one thought about endings or planned to manage their impact on people. Naturally concerned about the future, planners and implementers usually forget that people have to let go of the present first. They forget that while the first task of *change management* is to understand the destination and how to get there, the first task of *transition management* is to convince people to leave home. You'll save yourself a lot of grief if you remember that.

Managing Endings: A Checklist

Yes   No

____ ____   Have I studied the change carefully and identified who is likely to lose what—including what I myself am likely to lose?

____ ____ Do I understand the subjective realities of these losses to the people who experience them, even when they seem like overreaction to me?

____ ____ Have I acknowledged these losses with sympathy?

____ ____ Have I permitted people to grieve and publicly expressed my own sense of loss?

____ ____ Have I found ways to compensate people for their losses?

____ ____ Am I giving people accurate information and doing it again and again?

____ ____ Have I defined clearly what is over and what isn't?

____ ____ Have I found ways to "mark the ending"?

____ ____ Am I being careful not to denigrate the past but, when possible, to find ways to honor it?

____ ____ Have I made a plan for giving people a piece of the past to take with them?

____ ____ Have I made it clear how the ending we are making is necessary to protect the continuity of the organization or conditions on which the organization depends?

____ ____ Is the ending we are making big enough to get the job done in one step?

Final Questions

What actions can you take to help people deal more successfully with the endings that are taking place in your organization? What can you do today to get started on this aspect of transition management? (Write yourself a memo below.)

Chapter 4

Managing the Neutral Zone Successfully

It's not so much that we're afraid of change or so in love with the old ways, but it's that place in between that we fear. . . . It's like being between trapezes. It's Linus when his blanket is in the dryer. There's nothing to hold on to.

— Marilyn Ferguson, American futurist

One doesn't discover new lands without consenting to lose sight of the shore for a very long time.

— André Gide, French novelist

Just when you've decided that the hardest part of managing transition is getting people to let go of the old ways, you enter a state of affairs in which neither the old ways nor the new ways work satisfactorily. People are caught between the demands of conflicting systems and end up like immobilized Hamlets trying to decide whether "to be or not to be." Or all systems break down and it is (to use a client's memorable phrase) a time of "radio silence."

If this phase lasted only a short time, you could just wait for it to pass. But when the change is deep and far-reaching, this time between the old identity and the new can stretch out for months, even years. This, as Marilyn Ferguson says, is a time when you've let go of one trapeze with the faith that the new trapeze is on its way. In the meantime, there's nothing to hold on to.

A Very Difficult Time . . .

To make matters worse, your boss is probably getting impatient. "How long is it going to take you to implement those changes?" she asks, and you can tell from the tone in her voice that she thinks it has already taken too long. You wish you could say something positive, but you should be careful with promises. Frustration and tension are increasing, everyone seems to be moving at half speed, and you hear that some of the best people in the group have sent their resumés out.

Welcome to the middle phase of the transition process. This is a time Americans don't even have a name for. I call it the *neutral zone* because it is a nowhere between two somewheres. The neutral zone occurs in the lives of individuals, organizations, and even whole nations. As I write this, the Soviet Union and many of its former satellite countries are in the neutral zone. The dangers presented by the neutral zone take several forms:

1. Anxiety rises and motivation falls. People feel disoriented and self-doubting. They are resentful and self-protective. Energy is drained away from work into coping tactics. In one recent merger, managers in several key departments of the smaller company estimated that people's effectiveness had fallen 50%.

2. People in the neutral zone miss more workdays than at other times. The result is that, at best, productivity suffers and, at worst, medical and disability claims rise sharply. At a bank that was cutting back its workforce, absenteeism tripled. My firm had a terrible time scheduling transition management seminars because several key managers were on medical leaves.

3. Old weaknesses, long patched over or compensated for, reemerge in full flower. If customer service has always been a little weak, it's sure to fall apart in the neutral zone. That old resentment over generous executive severance packages will come up again, when everyone's trust in the organization's leaders is slipping. And that problem with the communication (or supervision or public relations) you thought was getting better suddenly gets very serious.

4. In the neutral zone personnel are overloaded, signals are often mixed, and systems are in flux and therefore unreliable. It is only natural that priorities get confused, information gets miscommunicated, and tasks go undone. It is also natural that with so many things uncertain and frustrating, turnover begins to rise.

5. Given the ambiguities of the neutral zone, it is natural for people to become polarized between those who want to rush forward and those who want to go back to the old ways. And given that polarization, it is natural

The crisis consists precisely in the fact that the old is dying and the new cannot be born. In this interregnum, a great variety of morbid symptoms appear.

Antonio Gramsci, political activist

Illness strikes men when they are exposed to change.

Herodotus, Greek historian

for consensus to break down and the level of discord to rise. Teamwork may be severely undermined, as may loyalty to the organization itself. Managed properly, this is only a temporary situation. Left unmanaged, it can lead to terminal chaos.

6. Finally, as Herodotus, the historian of a warlike age, would have been quick to note, corporations and other organizations are vulnerable to attack from outside. Disorganized and tired, people respond slowly and halfheartedly to competitive threats. They may even sabotage organizational responses to outside attacks.

It is for these reasons that managing the neutral zone is essential during a period of such enormous changes as our own. Neutral zone management isn't just something that would be nice if you had more time. It's the only way to ensure that the organization comes through the change intact and that those necessary changes actually work. The argument that there isn't time for such efforts is based on a serious misunderstanding of the situation: neutral zone management actually *saves* time in the long run because it means that you won't have to institute the change a second time when the first time didn't work. And it means that the organization won't come apart in the process of crossing the gap between the old way and the new.

. . . But Also a Creative Time

When everything is going smoothly, it's often hard to change things. "If it ain't broke," they say, "it don't need fixing." People who are sure they have the answers stop asking questions. And people who stop asking questions never challenge the status quo. Without such challenges, an organization can drift slowly into deep trouble before it gets a clear signal that something is wrong.

Often people from troubled organizations or outsiders who do not know much about the subject come up with the breakthrough answers. Such was the case with Henry Bessemer, the man who perfected the process of making steel by decarbonizing pig iron with heated air. He didn't know what he was doing, so, as he wrote, "I had an immense advantage over many others dealing with the problem. I had no fixed ideas derived from long-established practice to bias my mind, and did not suffer from the general belief that whatever is is right."[1]

Lacking clear systems and signals, the neutral zone is a chaotic time, but this lack is also the source of its positive aspect. Because the neutral zone

---

There is no squabbling so violent as that between people who accepted an idea yesterday and those who will accept the same idea tomorrow.

Christopher Morley, American writer

The interval between the decay of the old and the formation and the establishment of the new, constitutes a period of transition which must always necessarily be one of uncertainty, confusion, error, and wild and fierce fanaticism.

John C. Calhoun, American senator

The "silly question" is the first intimation of some totally new development.

Alfred North Whitehead

automatically puts people into Bessemer's situation, it is a time that is ripe with creative opportunity.

Your task is therefore twofold: first, to get your organization through in one piece and, second, to capitalize on the confusion by fostering innovation. We can take our motto for neutral zone management from the caption of a cartoon in which a little man sits in his car staring at a road sign: "Deep Doo-Doo, Next 750 Miles." The road through the neutral zone is indeed rough going, but it is passable if you're prepared for it. Here's what to do to help people make the journey.

Chaos often breeds life, while order breeds habit.

Henry Adams, American historian

"Normalize" the Neutral Zone

One of the most difficult aspects of the neutral zone for most people is that they don't understand it. They expect to be able to move straight from the old to the new. But this isn't a trip from one side of the street to the other. It's a journey from one identity to the other, and that takes time.

It takes nine months to have a baby, no matter how many people you put on the job.

American saying

The neutral zone is like the wilderness through which Moses led his people. That took 40 years, not because they were lost but because the generation that had known Egypt had to die off before they entered the Promised Land. If you take that literally, it is pretty discouraging: things won't really change until a whole generation of workers dies. On a less literal level, the point of Moses' long journey through the wilderness is entirely applicable to the organization: the outlook, attitudes, values, self-images, ways of thinking that had been functional in the past have to "die" before people are ready for life in the present. Moses made the ending when he led his people out of Egypt, but it was the 40 years in the neutral zone wilderness that *got Egypt out of his people*. It won't take you 40 years, but you aren't going to be able to do it quickly either.

Habit is habit, and not to be flung out of the window by any man, but coaxed downstairs a step at a time.

Mark Twain, American writer

The neutral zone isn't just meaningless waiting and confusion—it is a time when a necessary reorientation and redefinition is taking place, and people need to understand that. It is the winter during which the spring's new growth is taking shape under the earth.

People need to recognize that it is natural to feel somewhat frightened and confused in this no-man's-land. As the old patterns die in their minds and the new ones begin to take shape, people in the neutral zone are assailed by self-doubt and misgivings about their leaders. Ambiguity increases, and so does the longing for answers. That is why people in the neutral zone are so prone to follow anyone who seems to know where he or she is going—

Confusion is a word we have invented for an order which is not yet understood.

Henry Miller, American novelist

which, unfortunately, includes troublemakers and people who are heading toward the exits. No wonder the neutral zone is a time when turnover increases. (Moses even had that problem himself, although in his day it was called worshiping strange gods.)

Redefine It

Sometimes it's valuable to change the metaphor people are using to describe this uncomfortable time. In a manufacturing plant that was being closed, people were talking about the interim between the announcement and the closure as a time when the ship was sinking. Needless to say, that metaphor encouraged them to get off the vessel as fast as they could, and the company—which was counting on the output of the plant until it actually closed—found itself facing the possibility that production at the facility would collapse long before the company was ready for it to stop.

They needed a new metaphor, one that would have less disruptive implications for productivity. So they redefined the situation, accounting for the distress people were feeling by describing the neutral zone and then emphasizing the positive aspect of the situation by talking about "the last voyage" of the ship, not its sinking. This last voyage was a time during which both the organization and the individual could benefit. The organization needed the plant's output, and the individuals could use the time to improve their vocational marketability through skills enhancement, career strategies training, and experience-building reassignments.

When, in the new metaphor, the ship "reached port," everyone could "disembark" in a planned fashion, better for having stayed aboard and with the pride of a difficult job well done. It was no accident that, instead of falling as usually happens before a closure, output actually rose during the closing months of the plant's operation.

> *An adventure is only an inconvenience rightly understood. An inconvenience is only an adventure wrongly understood.*
>
> C. K. Chesterton, British writer

This may seem like playing with words: "sinking," "last voyage," "reaching port." But the words are labels on two very different packages, two different ways of looking at a difficult situation. Neither way invalidated the difficulty—that was a given. But one gave meaning to the situation, while the other left people feeling hopeless. One way of speaking said, "Make the most of this situation," while the other told people, "Get out of here as fast as you can."

Furthermore, the leadership of the factory and the corporate division that was depending on it did not merely talk in a new way. They put together training programs and reassignment policies that translated the words into actions people could see and profit from. They offered financial incentives for people to stay on board until their efforts were no longer needed, and they negotiated with other units in the corporation to hold positions open for those transferring until the factory was ready for them to go.

Create Temporary Systems for the Neutral Zone

What can you do to give structure and strength during a time when people are likely to feel lost and confused?

1. You can try hard to protect people from further changes while they're trying to regain their balance. You won't always succeed, of course—a new government regulation may be announced, a new product may be introduced by your main competitor, or the director of your department may be replaced. But many changes *can* be headed off or at least delayed. And if you cannot do so, you may be able to cluster the new change under a heading that relates it to the other changes you're going through. People can deal with a lot of change if it is coherent and part of a larger whole. But unrelated and unexpected changes, even if they are small ones, can be the proverbial straw that breaks the camel's back.

2. Next, review policies and procedures to see that they are adequate to deal with the confusing fluidity of the neutral zone. The "rules" under which you operate were set up to govern ongoing operations when things weren't changing as much as they are now. Do you need a new policy to cover some aspect of the new situation—a policy, for instance, about job classifications, priorities, time off for training, or who can make what kind of decision? Or do you need a new procedure for giving people temporary assignments, processing the work or handling overloads, identifying training needs, or scheduling meetings?

3. Consider a related question: What new roles, reporting relationships, or configurations of the organization chart do you need to develop to get through this time in the wilderness? (Moses, with the help of Jethro, the first organizational development consultant in history, reorganized his decision-making process in the neutral zone by regrouping people into new units under temporary, new "managers.") Hierarchy often breaks down in the neutral zone, and mixed groupings, like task forces and project teams,

"Listen, Moses. You've got too many people reporting to you. We're never going to get to the Promised Land if you don't delegate some power!"

Jethro (very loosely paraphrased)

are often very effective. People may have to be given temporary titles or made "acting" managers.

4. You will do well to set short-range goals for people to aim toward and to establish checkpoints along the way toward longer-term outcomes that you are seeking. This is a time when people get discouraged easily. Nothing seems to be happening in the neutral zone most of the time. It is important to give people a sense of achievement and of movement, even if you have to stretch the point a bit. This will help to counter the feelings of being lost, of meaninglessness, and of self-doubt that are common in the neutral zone.

5. Don't set people up for failure by promising high levels of productivity while you are in the neutral zone. Everyone loses when you fail to reach such ambitious targets: You look bad, people's self-confidence falls even further, and your superiors are upset. You may need to educate your superiors to get them to see that success at a lower level, which builds people up, is worth far more in the long run than failure at a higher level, which tears them down. Upper management hates to look bad, so help them to see the importance of setting realistic output objectives.

6. Find out what supervisors and managers need to learn to function successfully in the neutral zone, and then provide special training programs in those subjects. These may include seminars in problem solving, team building, group facilitation, and transition management tactics.

Strengthen Intragroup Connections

The neutral zone is a lonely place. People feel isolated, especially if they don't understand what is happening to them. As I have already noted, old problems are likely to surface and old resentments are likely to come to life again. For these reasons it is especially important to try to rebuild a sense of identification with the group and of connectedness with one another.

At a large aerospace facility that was being reorganized, connections were established through weekly lunches that, in the course of a year, put representatives from every group together with the general manager of the site for an informal meal. During the lunch the GM answered all questions and gathered suggestions for changes in policy that would help people deal with the "wilderness." Week after week, people returned to the project teams and departmental units with a new level of trust in and a greater feeling of connectedness with their leader.

At a food processing plant, the leadership wanted a faster way to involve everyone, and so a Family Day was planned. The factory was shut down for a day, and everyone came together at a local theme park, where a large area had been rented for their gathering. Events were planned that mixed levels of authority and which blended groups that were sometimes polarized by their different daily functions. Managers worked hard to meet and reassure the families of the people who worked for them. The results were clear the next morning—there was less anxiety and more solidarity between exempt and nonexempt workers.

Communications help to keep people feeling included in and connected to the organization. Many companies have used newsletters as a way of maintaining contact with, and showing concern for, employees in the neutral zone. In the neutral zone there is often very little new information of the sort that produces public announcements and memos. Without a communication channel that is appropriate to a time of worry and waiting, rumors multiply and people alternate between anxiety and apathy.

In one corporation that was relocating its headquarters, the *Transition News* kept everyone abreast of progress, squelched rumors, and featured articles on schools, health care, shopping, real estate, and other aspects of the new location. A "Letters to the Editor" section answered questions.

At the Santa Clara, California, Intel fabricating plant, the newsletter explained the job-posting system and described upcoming job search seminars. It also announced barbecues for several shifts and carried farewell messages from departing personnel.

At the Cheboygan, Michigan, Procter & Gamble paper products plant, a newsletter was used very effectively to maintain contact with employees during long months of uncertainty while the plant was being shut down. It was a folksy update on people who had found positions at other P & G plants, an advice column by the local employee assistance program specialist (who termed himself a transition counselor), news stories about the progress of the "yearbook" that was being created to record everyone's final year, and ads for the sale of cars, appliances, and prom dresses.

In each case a newsletter was effectively used to keep in touch with people during a time when they tend to feel confused and disconnected. And, not coincidentally, all three organizations made it through the neutral zone without the lasting damage that many organizations suffer there.

Be wary of showing preferences. In the neutral zone people want to feel they are "all in this boat together"—another good metaphor. They will put up with a lot of discomfort if *everyone* must do so. But if there are people who, because of their position or other advantages, are getting special treatment, there may be trouble. That trouble can even be sparked by perquisites that individuals have always enjoyed. First-class air travel for upper-level managers, special parking spaces for staff members, and an executive dining room can all loom large as resentment-building symbols of privilege and an unwitting message that some people have it easy during a difficult time when the rank and file is suffering.

Use a Transition Monitoring Team

One of the persistent problems during transition is for decision makers and those implementing decisions to be clear on precisely what impact the decisions and actions will have. Leaders usually assume that all the feedback they will need will come up through regular channels and will be voiced at staff meetings in reply to the question, "How are things going?" Such is seldom the case. The answers to that innocent question are distorted by being filtered and interpreted and sometimes blocked on their way upward. Ed Carlson, the former CEO of United Airlines, used to call it the NETMA problem— Nobody Ever Tells Me Anything.

This is where a transition monitoring team is valuable. The TMT, as it is often called, is a group of 7 to 12 people chosen from as wide a cross-section of the organization as possible. It meets every week or two to take the pulse of the organization in transition. It has no decision-making power and is not intended to suggest courses of action. Rather, its purpose is to facilitate upward communication and to do three other things:

1. The TMT demonstrates that the organization wants to know how things are going for people.

2. The TMT is an effective focus group to review plans or communications before they are announced.

3. The TMT provides a point of ready access to the organization's grapevine and so can be used to correct misinformation and counter rumors.

Note a few warnings about using TMTs. First, make sure that the mission of the group is clear. Second, don't give the function to an existing group of upper-level managers; set up a special group, and make sure it represents different constituencies within the organization. Third, ensure that the TMT has access to the organization's leadership by including someone in the group who has the leader's ear. Finally, make sure that the concerns voiced by the group don't disappear; report back to the group regularly what is being done with the issues being raised, and be sure that at least some of them will lead to visible actions.

Using the Neutral Zone Creatively

If you have always done it that way, it is probably wrong.

Charles Kettering, American inventor

While it is essential to build into the neutral zone temporary systems for getting people through the wilderness intact, you need to do more. You need to capitalize on the opportunity that the neutral zone provides to do things differently and better.

In the neutral zone restraints on innovation are the weakest. Every organizational system has its own natural "immune system" whose task it is to resist novelty. That is not bad, per se. If the organization didn't have such an immune system, every "germ" of change would take root, and the organization would not have enough stability to get anything done or enough continuity to give people the identity they need. But such necessities carry a price tag.

The cost of an immune system is that even good germs get filtered out or killed off. The old immune system choked off creativity in its own manner, and no matter how loose and free the new way of doing things is, its immune system will assume a form that makes creativity difficult in some different way. It is during *the gap between the old and the new* that the organization's systems of immunity are weak enough to let truly creative solutions emerge unhampered. Only when the old way of seeing things disappears are habit patterns broken, and a new way will emerge.

Innovation will take place automatically in the neutral zone if you provide people with the temporary structures discussed above, and if you encourage them to find new ways to do things. Here are some ways in which you can actively encourage creativity.[2]

First, establish by word and example that this is a time to step back and take stock, a time to question the "usual," and a time to come up with new and creative solutions to the organization's difficulties. Explain how business as usual chokes off creativity and that the present is the best possible time to generate and test new ideas. Model this new manner by taking time to step back and question how your own job is done. Review those policies and procedures over which you have control.

Second, provide opportunities for others to do the same: schedule retreats, policy reviews, surveys, and suggestion campaigns. Be sure to plan into each of these efforts a way to keep people informed about what is being done with the ideas generated and the suggestions made. Nothing undermines an effort like this faster than the appearance of good ideas being forgotten or not taken seriously.

Third, provide training in the techniques of discovery and innovation. This is the time for creative thinking courses and workshops on innovation. Such efforts usually fail to bear fruit, not because they are poorly done but because they are ill-timed. They take place when the immune system is too strong. Now is the time to try them again. Some people simply don't know how to get out of their rut. Help them.

Fourth, encourage experiment. People always have ideas that they have been wishing they had the chance to try. People naturally generate solutions to problems they've been living with. What they seldom do without encouragement and support is to try their ideas. Too often experimentation seems to people a risky undertaking that requires someone's blessing. Give it yours. You'll be surprised how many improvements are just waiting for the chance to happen.

Fifth, embrace losses, setbacks, or disadvantages as entry points for new solutions. Steve Jobs and Steve Wozniak built their first Apple PC because they lacked the money to buy the computer-building kits that were "the right way" to build a computer in those days. Yamaha turned the sagging market for grand pianos into a challenge to come up with an electronic instrument that mimics the sound and touch of the big piano perfectly. Brother took the deteriorating sewing machine market as a challenge to move into typewriters and other electronic instruments. Louisiana Pacific Corporation, which lacks the big timber stands of its major competitors, turned that lack to its advantage by shifting to the manufacture of boards and sheets made of gypsum and recycled paper.

Sixth, look for opportunities to brainstorm new answers to old problems. You have lived with them for so long that you may have unwittingly given up any hope of solving them. Break through this block, not by finding the single right answer but by finding 10 or 20 new answers—the crazier the better.

Finally, restrain the natural impulse in times of ambiguity and disorganization to push prematurely for certainty and closure. It is tempting to rally around "everyone pulling together" in the neutral zone, but you can do that only at the cost of finding a new direction to pull in. Be careful that your efforts to build solidarity and a sense of belonging don't unintentionally squeeze out dissent. You may even need to appoint a devil's advocate or an

---

To exist is to change, to change is to mature, to mature is to go on creating oneself endlessly.

Henri Bergson, French philosopher

When choosing between two evils, I always like to try the one I've never tried before.

Mae West, American actress

The way to get good ideas is to get lots of ideas and throw the bad ones away.

Linus Pauling, American chemist

official critic of apparent consensus to see that people don't choke off new ideas in their desire to keep the team in one piece.

In doing these things, you will achieve the gain that helps offset and justify the pain of the neutral zone. Too much work in organizations today is being done on the model of the bucket brigade, the nineteenth-century fire-fighting system in which water in separate containers was passed hand-to-hand from its source, down a row of people, to be thrown on the fire by the last person in line. That human chain was only as strong as its weakest member. If Charlie had to keep setting down the buckets to rest, they didn't reach the thrower quickly enough. But Charlie wasn't the only problem. Every time a bucket was handed from one person to another, a little of the water would slop over the edge. After 50 handoffs, the water level was likely to be low. Finally, there was the problem of delivery. In the bucket brigade, the water would reach only as high or as far as the last person could toss it. There was no power being developed within the system to push the water up and out to the flames at a distance.

So it is with modern bucket brigade work systems: Each piece of work is done by an individual, and there is no system power being built up. When the same individuals (or even half their number) hold a fire hose, there is a power being harnessed that pushes the water out the end and up to the third or fourth floor.

Whatever the details of the situation you face, the question to ask yourself is, "How can I make this interim between the old and the new not only a bearable time but a time during which the organization and everyone's place in it is enhanced? How can we come out of this waiting time better than we were before the transition began?" Here are some examples of using the neutral zone creatively.

When you shift from one technological system to another, use the interim to redesign the work flow so that you aren't simply improving the technological means to an unimproved end.

When another company acquires yours, clarify your team's mission and improve its functioning to maximize the chances that when the dust clears, it will be viewed as essential to the success of the acquiring company.

When you restructure your department, involve everyone in a no-holds-barred session of creative problem solving in which roles are redefined and procedures are redesigned.

The generic advice is to turn setbacks into chances to improve things. The motto might be: "When orders fall, set people to work painting the factory."

Where all think alike, no one thinks very much.

Walter Lippmann, American journalist

It is easier to get forgiveness than it is to secure permission.

Jesuit saying

And don't bog down in getting everyone's blessing for your interim project. Such things are validated by their good results, and the good results are so much better than those of inaction that blessings almost always follow.

The key to succeeding in these efforts is to look at the neutral zone as a chance to do something new and interesting—and to pursue that goal with energy and courage.

To equip your people to take advantage of the neutral zone opportunity for innovation, you need to foster a spirit of entrepreneurship among them. That spirit is totally alien to the "do what you're told" mood that characterizes many organizations, but an entrepreneurial outlook is the surest antidote to becoming frightened by change. It is entrepreneurial opportunism that spells the difference between success and failure in using the neutral zone creatively, and this opportunism depends on a willingness to take risks. That willingness, in turn, is not likely to develop without an organizational tolerance for intelligently conceived ventures that fail. In an organization that punishes failure, regardless of the value of the effort that failed, you aren't going to get this kind of effort. Watch out particularly that valuable concepts like "excellence" or "zero defects" don't get used as excuses to punish intelligent failures.

Entrepreneurs see change as the norm and as healthy. Usually they do not bring about the change themselves. But—and this defines entrepreneur and entrepreneurship—the **entrepreneur always searches for change, responds to it, and exploits it as opportunity.**

Peter Drucker, Management writer

Hardly a work project or procedure going on today in an American organization could not be better designed. In some sectors of the economy, it's all bucket brigades and no hoses. Yet most efforts at getting "lean and mean" represent little more than sending half the bucket brigade home and telling the rest to speed up their efforts. A better answer is to use the time in the neutral zone creatively as an opportunity to redesign how you do what you do. If you do that, you will emerge from the wilderness both stronger and better adapted to your new environment. Neutral zone creativity is the key to turning transition from a time of breakdown to a time of breakthrough.

A Final Note on the Neutral Zone

When old words die out on the tongue, new melodies break forth from the heart; and where the old tracks are lost, new country is revealed with its wonders.

Rabindranath Tagore, Indian philosopher

Behind all this advice is an idea that can be validated with dozens of examples from both organizations and individual lives. During this apparently uneventful journey through the wilderness, a significant change takes place within people—or if it doesn't, the change isn't likely to produce the results it is intended to. That change represents a kind of inner "sorting" process in which old and no longer appropriate habits are discarded and newly appropriate patterns of thought and action are developed.

In his book, *Muddling Through*, Roger Golde tells a story that might stand as a fable about how this sorting goes on in the neutral zone if the circumstances permit it. The story concerns a French Army unit that was isolated in the Sahara desert during World War II. Resupplying them was terribly difficult, and they were running out of everything. Their clothes were in particularly awful shape. Somehow a Red Cross clothing shipment reached them, but most of the clothes were used with size labels illegible or missing, and everyone wondered how they could be assigned to the people they would most nearly fit.

The commander, obviously an expert on neutral zone strategies, simply lined the troops up and issued each man one shirt, one pair of pants, and two shoes—with no attempt to fit for size or even to match pairs. Then he shouted, *"Debrouillez-vous!"* which means roughly, "Sort them out." There was an enormous thrashing and rumbling while the men switched and swapped until they had clothes that would more or less fit them. The result was a very adequate solution to an impossible problem—except for one unlucky soldier who ended up with two left shoes.

This is merely to illustrate that people can work out much of the necessary business of the neutral zone if you will protect them, encourage them, and give them the structures and opportunities they need to do it.

Let's call that the neutral zone password *Debrouillez-vous!*

Managing the Neutral Zone: A Checklist

Yes   No

____ ____   Have I done my best to normalize the neutral zone by explaining it as an uncomfortable time which, with careful attention, can be turned to everyone's advantage?

____ ____   Have I redefined it by choosing a new and more affirmative metaphor with which to describe it?

____ ____   Have I reinforced that metaphor with training programs, policy changes, and financial rewards for people to keep doing their jobs during the neutral zone?

____ ____   Am I protecting people adequately from further changes?

____ ____   If I can't protect them, am I clustering those changes meaningfully?

____ ____   Have I created the temporary policies and procedures that we need to get us through the neutral zone?

____ ____   Have I created the temporary roles, reporting relationships, and organizational groupings that we need to get us through the neutral zone?

____ ____   Have I set short-range goals and checkpoints?

____ ____   Have I set realistic output objectives?

____ ____   Have I found what special training programs we need to deal successfully with the neutral zone?

____ ____   Have I found ways to keep people feeling that they still belong to the organization and are valued by our part of it? And have I taken care that perks and other forms of "privilege" are not undermining the solidarity of the group?

____ ____   Have I set up a transition monitoring team to keep realistic feedback flowing upward during the time in the neutral zone?

____ ____   Are my people willing to experiment and take risks in intelligently conceived ventures—or are we punishing all failures?

____ ____   Have I stepped back and taken stock of how things are being done in my part of the organization? (This is worth doing both for its own sake and as a visible model for others' similar behavior.)

____ ____   Have I provided others with opportunities to do the same thing? Have I provided them with the resources—facilitators, survey instruments, and so on—that will help them do that?

____ ____   Have I seen to it that people build their skills in creative thinking and innovation?

____ ____   Have I encouraged experiment and seen to it that people are not punished for failing in intelligent efforts that did not pan out?

____ ____   Have I worked to transform the losses of our organization into opportunities to try doing things a new way?

____ ____   Have I set an example by brainstorming many answers to my old problems—the ones that people say you just have to live with? Am I encouraging others to do the same?

—— ——   Am I regularly checking to see that I am not pushing for certainty and closure where it would be more conducive to creativity to live a little longer with uncertainty and questions?

—— ——   Am I using my time in the neutral zone as an opportunity to replace bucket brigades with integrated systems throughout the organization?

Final Questions

What actions can you take to help people deal more successfully with the neutral zone in which your organization currently finds itself? What can you do today to get started on this aspect of transition management? (Write yourself a memo below.)

---

[1] John Gardner and Francesca Gardner Reese, eds. *Quotations of Wit and Wisdom* (New York: W. W. Norton, 1975).

[2] If you want to know more about creativity—a vast subject in itself—here are some of the books I have found useful:

James L. Adams, *Conceptual Blockbusting* (Reading, MA: Addison-Wesley, 1986).

William J. J. Gordon, *Synectics* (New York: Collier Books, 1961).

William C. Miller, *The Creative Edge* (Reading, MA: Addison-Wesley, 1987).

Roger von Oech, *A Whack on the Side of the Head* (New York: Warner Books, 1990).

Chapter 5

Launching a New Beginning

The only joy in the world is to begin.

— Cesare Pavese, Italian writer

The world fears a new experience more than it fears anything. Because a new experience displaces so many old experiences. . . . The world doesn't fear a new idea. It can pigeon-hole any idea. But it can't pigeon-hole a real new experience.

— D. H. Lawrence, English novelist

Beginnings are psychological phenomena, not simply practical ones. In practical terms, things change quickly: When the old computers were carted away and the new system was installed, everyone started to get along without them. When the budget was cut, people started immediately to work under new financial constraints. When they put the new organization chart on the wall, individuals knew what their new roles were, who their new bosses were, with whom they worked. In terms of the situational change, a new start had been made.

But those were only starts. The transition was still under way, and people were still in the neutral zone feeling lost, confused, and uncertain. The beginning took place only after they had come through the wilderness and were ready to make the emotional commitment to do things the new way and see themselves as new people. Starts involve new situations. Beginnings involve new understandings, new values, new attitudes, and—most of all—new identities.

Beginnings are always messy.

John Galsworthy, English novelist

Starts can and should be carefully designed, like an object. Beginnings can and should be nurtured, like a plant. Starts take place on a schedule as a result of decisions. They are signaled by announcements: "On March 25, the twenty-four district branches will be consolidated into six regional offices." Beginnings, on the other hand, are the final phase of the organic process that I call "transition," and their timing is not measured in the dates written on an implementation schedule: Beginnings follow the timing of the mind and heart.

The change management plan will spell out the details of the start, but it will very likely assume that the beginning will happen automatically. Bosses always seem to assume the same thing, as they demonstrate when they say impatiently, "You guys have had *two weeks* to get the new computer system [or the new self-managed teams, etc.] up and going! Your people don't seem to be *with it*. What's the problem?" They're confusing starts with beginnings.

Ambivalence Toward Beginnings

Beginnings are strange things. People want them to happen but fear them at the same time. After the long and seemingly pointless wanderings through the neutral zone, most people are greatly relieved to arrive at whatever Promised Land they've been seeking. Yet beginnings are also scary, for they are the time to make a new commitment and actually be the new person that the new situation demands. Beginnings feel frightening to most of us for a number of reasons.

First, beginnings reactivate some of the old anxieties that were originally triggered by the ending. Beginnings, after all, establish once and for all that an ending was real. I may, for example, have decided to leave my old career, but until I begin working at a new career, there is something provisional about the decision. The new beginning ratifies the ending. (That finality is paradoxically also the source of excitement, for it signals that you've made a clean break and have the chance to begin again from scratch.)

Every beginning is a consequence. Every beginning ends something.
Paul Valery

Second, the new way of doing things represents a gamble: There is always the possibility it won't work. The very idea of doing something the new way may be crazy, or it may be unrealistic to think that a particular organization can carry it off. Even if it does work, there is the possibility that the individual in question won't be good enough at it to succeed, or even that he or she will make a shameful mess of the effort.

Third is the way in which the prospect of a risky new beginning resonates with the past. On a personal level, it may trigger old memories of failures that destroyed the individual's self-esteem. Organizationally, it may resonate with a history in which failures have been punished or with a particular incident in which a new beginning was aborted in some traumatic fashion.

One of the greatest pains to human nature is the pain of a new idea.
Walter Bagehot, English political scientist

Finally, for some people new beginnings destroy what was a pleasant experience in the neutral zone. Most people don't like the wilderness, but a few find ambiguity and the slower pace of work rather pleasant. The confusion gives them a cover under which to conceal their own lack of interest in the tasks at hand, and the absence of a clear agenda gives them an excuse for their inactivity. For such people, the new beginning is an end to a pleasant holiday from accountability and pressure.

The Timing of New Beginnings

Like any organic process, beginnings cannot be made to happen by a word or act. They happen when the timing of the transition process allows them to happen, just as flowers and fruit appear on a schedule that is natural and not subject to anyone's will. That is why it is so important to understand the transition process and where people are in it.

There go my people. I must find out where they are going so that I can lead them.

Alexandre Ledru-Rollin, French politician

Only when you get into people's shoes and feel what they are feeling can you help them to manage their transition. More beginnings abort because they were not preceded by well-managed endings and neutral zones than for any other reason.

But if beginnings cannot be forced according to one's personal wishes, they can be encouraged, supported, and reinforced. You can't turn the key or flip the switch, but you can cultivate the ground and provide the nourishment. What you can do falls under four headings:

1. You can explain the basic *purpose* behind the outcome you seek. People have to understand the logic of it before they turn their minds to work on it.

2. You can paint a *picture* of how the outcome will look and feel. People need to experience it imaginatively before they can give their hearts to it.

3. You can lay out a step-by-step *plan* for phasing in the outcome. People need a clear idea of how they can get where they need to go.

4. You can give each person a *part* to play in both the plan and the outcome itself. People need a tangible way to contribute and participate.

Do unto others as they would be done unto.

Proverbial advice, modified

To make a new beginning, people need The Four P's: the purpose, a picture, the plan, and a part to play. For any particular individual, one or sometimes two of these P's will predominate. You probably have a dominant need yourself, which means that you will tend to stress that thing when you communicate with others. Naturally, you think that others approach beginnings the way you do—which isn't necessarily so. So it is important to remember to cover all four of these bases when you talk about the new beginning you want to help people make.

Clarify and Communicate the Purpose

What is the idea behind what you're doing? The idea behind Moses' journey through the wilderness was that his people had been persecuted in their adopted home of Egypt. The idea of a land of their own, a place promised to them by their God, was something everyone could understand. It was a solution to problems they experienced. It was an answer to the question, "Why are we doing this?" It represented a clear purpose for their journey.

You need to explain the purpose behind the new beginning clearly. You may discover that people do not have a realistic idea of where the organization really stood and what its problems were. In that case, you need to sell problems before you try to sell solutions. If this wasn't done during the ending phase, you'll have to provide answers to these questions:

What was the problem?

Who said so, and on what evidence?

What would have occurred if no one had acted to solve it?

What would have happened to us if that had occurred?

There is always a purpose behind a change, though sometimes you will need to adapt the idea to the interests and understandings of your audience. An increase in shareholder value is not an idea that means much to rank-and-file workers, unless it is translated into things that could affect their security, pay, or working conditions. The same is true for such important ideas as quality improvement, customer satisfaction, and increased profitability.

One of the terrible obstacles to many beginnings is that there is *no discernible purpose behind the proposed changes.* There are different reasons for that state of affairs, and each of them calls for a different action from you.

1. *The purpose is not discernible because it has not yet been clearly explained in terms that mean something to you.*

   That may be because it was not effectively communicated or because you simply did not understand. In either case, ask for more explanation, making it clear that you are not questioning the intent but that you need more help in communicating it to your people.

   It may also be because it has not been thought through clearly enough to be effectively communicated. You should ask for more explanation, as in the previous case—though this time the result may be more tricky because the leaders may have to face the fact that they aren't yet clear themselves.

If you cry forward, you must make clear the direction in which to go. Don't you see that if you fail to do that and simply call out the word to a monk and a revolutionary, they will go in precisely the opposite directions.

Anton Chekhov, Russian dramatist

Great minds have purposes, others have wishes.

Washington Irving, American essayist

2. *The purpose is not discernible because it has not been communicated at all. This time there may be three reasons:*

There may be no purpose, at least none that will stand up to scrutiny. It may be a whim. It may be an attempt to show that the leadership is not passive. It may be because the organization next door did it. It may be the result of drawing straws in the boardroom. If you decide there isn't a valid purpose behind the change, you aren't likely to be able to bring people out of the neutral zone. Circle the wagons and figure how best to use your time until the decision-making process gets back on track.

There is an idea, but the leadership isn't talking because they don't think people need to understand. At least not now. Ultimately leaders who take this approach lose their followers. If you're lucky, it will be sooner rather than later. But in the meantime, if feedback to your superiors has no effect, follow the advice given in the foregoing paragraph.

There is a purpose—at least you strongly suspect there is—but the "official reason" is a smoke screen to cover what cannot publicly be said. The technical term for this is "lying," and its long-term effects on people are very bad. They lose trust, withdraw their loyalty, and grow resentful. At best, their effort falls. At worst, they begin looking for ways to pay the organization back. What can you do? Often, not much. But sometimes you can get your company's executives to see that the truth is not as terrifying as they imagine. Sometimes you can help them figure out how to tell the truth—or at least stop lying—without wrecking everything. Failing that, you can try, without slitting your own throat, to disengage yourself from the lying.

Sometimes you may find yourself falling back on the age-old explanation, "The boss wants us to do it," or "if we don't do it, we're all fired." Few organizations run for long on such purposes, but those sentiments are strong motivators—at least for short bursts of activity.

Perhaps the situation is not so dark as in the foregoing scenarios. Let's assume, for example, that you're involved in the decision making and so have some influence in setting and defining the purpose behind the action. Bear these things in mind:

The purpose must be real, not make-believe. When budget cuts are described as a way to "improve operations" (as they were in an organization where my firm recently worked), you're simply sowing mistrust and cynicism at a time when you're going to need all the commitment and energy you can muster.

The second is that the purpose needs to grow out of the situation faced by the organization and the organization's nature and resources. Today many different purposive ideas are fashionable:

"We're going for *excellence.*"

"We're going to be a *cutting-edge* company."

"We're going to be *Number One* in the industry."

"We're going to be the *low-cost producer* or *value-added* leader or *customer-service* champ."

These are clichés. The words mean something, but the speakers who use them usually do not. If they did, they would say what they mean and not what everyone else is saying these days. When SAS Airlines said that customer service was the key, when Ford said that quality was the key, when any organization says what its own leadership really believes, everyone listens. But when organizations simply repeat some currently widely touted purposive idea, all the employees hear is, "me too."

The purpose that you need to launch a new beginning must come from within the organization—from its will, abilities, resources, and character. To be more specific, it must come with how these inherent qualities interact with the situation in which the organization finds itself. It is that interaction that spells opportunity in a changing world. If this purpose is simply copied from another organization, or if it belies the real situation in which the organization finds itself, it won't do its job. Successful new beginnings are based on a clear and appropriate purpose. Without one, there may be lots of starts but no real beginnings. Without a beginning, the transition is incomplete. And without transition, the change changes nothing.

Just because everything is different doesn't mean that anything has changed.

Irene Peter, American epigrammatist

After a Purpose, a Picture

Purposes are critical to beginnings, but they are rather abstract. They are *ideas,* and most people are not ready to throw themselves into a difficult and risky undertaking simply on the basis of an idea.[1] They need something they can see, at least in their imaginations. They need a *picture* of how the outcome will look, and they need to be able to imagine how it will feel to be a participant in it.

This picture in people's heads is the reality they live in, and one of the losses that takes place during the ending phase of a transition is that the old picture—the mental image of how and why things are the way they are—falls apart. Much of the pain of the neutral zone comes from the fact that it is a time without a viable organizational picture. (Part of the task of neutral zone management is to create a "temporary wilderness" picture in people's minds, a picture that explains and validates what they are experiencing.) It is the new organizational picture that refocuses people's energies and brings them out of the neutral zone with a new sense of their collective identity and a new meaning for their efforts.

So your second task is to create this picture.[2] There is nothing mystical or artistic about this process. Moses, who was so self-doubting about his ability to inspire others that he tried to turn down Jehovah's call to lead the Jewish people, did it very effectively. He translated the *idea* of a Promised Land into the *picture* of a Land of Milk and Honey. He did not stop with creating an understanding of the destination; he portrayed the destination in a way that engaged their imaginations.

This change that you are trying to manage—what is the outcome going to look like and sound like? How are people going to get their work done and interact with each other? What is the spatial layout of the place going to be like? How is a day going to be organized? When a person first encounters the new way of doing things, what is going to be the impression it makes—the feeling a person gets just from being there? In other words, what are people going to *experience* that is going to be different?

Use visual aids to convey the picture of the new way things will be. A floorplan of the new office layout, a picture of the new automated packaging line, a video of a self-managed team planning the coming month's priorities, a map showing the expanded area served by the branches of the merged banks—these aids help people to imagine what the new way will be like. Another way to paint a picture is to arrange for people to visit another organization where things are already done in the new way. As they see and talk with people like themselves working successfully under the new conditions, they can begin to visualize and feel at home with the new way.

Two Things to Watch Out For

A couple of warnings about helping your people visualize the new way. First, don't expect the picture to have its effect prematurely—that is, before your people have made an ending and let go of the past. There is no harm (and there is actual gain) in showing the picture to people as soon as the change is

A rock pile ceases to be a rock pile the moment a single man contemplates it, bearing within him the image of a cathedral.

Antoine de Saint-Exupéry, French novelist

announced. Doing so will plant the picture of the future in their imaginations, where it will reassure them. But it does not make the transition happen. It was not the image of the Land of Milk and Honey that got the people out of Egypt or through the wilderness to the Promised Land—it was Moses' skill as a transition manager.

Misplaced faith in the picture's power to make a transition happen is encouraged by a misunderstanding that is common among people who have designed change projects. Such people typically go through *their* transitions before they launch the changes, while they're still struggling with the problems and searching for solutions. By the time they have announced the change, they have long since put the ending and the neutral zone behind them and are ready for a new beginning. But they forget that middle management is probably just entering the neutral zone and that the rank and file have not yet even made their endings.

This situation might be called "the marathon effect"—it is similar to what happens in road races with thousands of runners. The front runners take off like rabbits, then the second rank (who are a little slower anyway) start running, and then the middle ranks (who are nowhere near as fast) get under way. By the time the leaders are well out on the course, the Sunday runners in the rear, who were too far back even to hear the starting gun (and who only hope to be able to finish the race) are beginning to stir. A rumor comes back through the crowd: the race has started. The Sunday runners move their feet a little to loosen up, but they can't get moving yet. They shuffle a little, then begin taking small steps.

About the time the Sunday runners have speeded up to a slow jog, some of the front runners are nearing the finish line and thinking, "Well, this is about over. Good race. What'll I do next week?" So it is with the company executives. They went through *their* transitions long ago when they started grappling with the problems. They forget that their followers are still struggling.

The second warning is not to overwhelm people with a picture that is so hard for them to identify with that they become intimidated rather than excited by it. One of my firm's clients presented a videotape of a new automated production line. The tape was made by a fancy outfit in Hollywood and featured stirring music from the broadcasts of the recently completed Los Angeles Olympic Games. The workers watched dramatic angle shots of their product speeding through space-age machinery, and they saw people studying computer printouts that they could not imagine understanding. The result was that most of the audience left thinking they couldn't do the work.

Hope is generally a wrong guide, though it is very good company by the way.

Charles Montagu, Earl of Halifax, British statesman

The same manufacturing plant got a much better result from a visual aid that cost perhaps a twentieth as much as the video. It was a wonderfully done scale model of the new, automated production line with little people and little cases of products that could be moved around. It was set up in the factory lunchroom, where workers could see it every day and even play with it. Before long the toy workers were tagged with the names of actual employees, and people were beginning to picture themselves at work in the new setting.

Now Create a Plan

Some people really respond to the picture. Once they get it in their heads, they will find a way to reach the destination that has captured their imagination. Many executives and planners fall into this group, and because they don't feel a personal need for a plan that spells out the details of the route from *here* to *there*, they underestimate how much others need such a plan. For many operationally minded people, the picture is interesting, but the real question is, "What do we do on Monday?"

The plan I am talking about is not the large-scale outline of stages and dates, which explains when, for example, the new automated machinery will be ordered, when it will arrive, when it will be installed, and when the first shipment of goods manufactured the new way will be shipped. That is the plan for the changes, not the transitions. The plan I am talking about outlines the steps and schedule in which people will receive the information, training, and support they will need to make the transition. It lays out the nature and timing of key events that mark the phases of the transition: a ceremony marking the closure of a facility or the disbanding of a group, the formation of a transition monitoring team, the scheduling of a visit to another site, an all-hands question-and-answer session with the site manager, the start of a training program, the date of a planning retreat or a brainstorming session, and the like.

The transition management plan differs from the change management plan in several ways. First, it is much more detailed, addressing the change on the personal rather than the collective level. It is much more person-oriented because it tells José, Sally, and Ray how and when their worlds are going to change. Second, it is oriented to the process and not just the outcome. It lays out the details of what's going to be done to help those individuals deal with the effects of the changes. It tells them when they can expect to receive information and training, and how and when they can have input into the planning process.

A third difference is less evident in the final product but is important in its creation. A change management plan starts with the outcome and then works backward, step by step, to create the necessary preconditions for that outcome. A transition management plan, on the other hand, starts with where people are and then works forward, step by step, through the process of leaving the past behind, getting through the wilderness and profiting from it, and emerging with new attitudes, behaviors, and identity. A transition management plan can be put together by selecting, designing, and scheduling events, actions, and projects from the possibilities that are listed in chapters 3, 4, and 5.

Finally, a Part to Play

Plans are immensely reassuring to most people, not just because they contain information but because they exist. As is noted in the Book of Exodus, in the wilderness of the neutral zone people "murmured." One of the things they must have murmured was, "Do you think Moses has any *plan*, or do you think he's making this up as he goes along?" The existence of the plan sends a message: somebody is looking after us, taking our needs seriously, and watching out so we don't get lost along the way.

But even the best-laid plans leave a troubling doubt in the minds of some people. They don't see *their* names on the wall chart. No one has told them how *they* fit into the new scheme of things. No one has given *them* any role to play in the journey itself. The purpose, the picture, and the plan all omit something: a part for them to play. Until that is provided, many people will feel left out and will find it difficult to make a new beginning.

You'll usually need to give people two parts to play. First, they need to see the role and their relationship to others in the new scheme of things. If your name appears on the new organization chart, you may not like where they put you, but it beats not seeing your name on the chart at all. Until people know the parts they are to play, they can't begin the slow process of adjusting their hopes and fears to the new reality. Until they know their parts, fantasies dictate their actions and can lead them far from the new realities they will be facing.

But that is only the part people will play in the *outcome*. You also need to give people a role in dealing effectively with the transition process itself. The easiest way to do this is to be sure that everyone has a place on a planning task force, climate survey group, problem-solving circle, or transition monitoring team. If this is not possible, set up formal input systems for such groupings so that each person has at least an indirect part to play in the transition management process. This is particularly important for people who have lost a significant part in the old order. (See the section in chapter 3 entitled "Compensate for the Losses.")

Giving people a significant part to play in the transition management process facilitates the new beginning in five ways:

1. It gives people new insight into the real problems being faced by the organization as it comes out of the neutral zone and redefines itself. When people understand problems, they are in the market for solutions.

2. By sharing these problems, you align yourself and your subordinates on one side and the problems on the other. The polarity is not between you and them; you are allies, not adversaries. If relationships have been frayed by change, this is a chance to rebuild them.

3. Giving people a part brings their firsthand knowledge to bear on solving problems. Joint decisions are not necessarily better than unilateral ones, but including people makes their knowledge available to the decision maker, whoever that may be.

4. The knowledge thus provided is more than the facts about the problem— it also includes the facts about the self-interest of the various parties in the situation. Outcomes work best if they serve (or at least don't violate) the self-interest of the participants. Without that knowledge, the results are likely to be solutions that, however technically or economically satisfactory, run afoul of human issues.

5. Finally, everyone who plays a part is implicitly implicated in the outcome. That is, after all, how democracy works: you vote, and your vote is an implicit promise to abide by the results. Although actual votes are rare in the organizational world, this essential strength of democracy is still attainable and advantageous. As in the political arena, it is more important that people accept the solution, whatever it is, than that it is the ideal solution. In most cases, excellence is about seven parts commitment and three parts strategy.

Reinforcing the New Beginning

All of these tactics help people to leave the disturbing and creative chaos of the neutral zone and refocus their energies in new directions. They help people to shape new identities to replace the ones they gave up when they let go of how things used to be. But that refocusing needs to be reinforced if it is to keep its new shape and not revert to chaos when the initial focus is confronted by the continuing stream of changes that are sure to come along.[3]

Rule One: Be Consistent

The first form of reinforcement is consistency of message. Every policy, procedure, and list of priorities sends a message, but if you aren't careful, your messages will be conflicting ones.

If you say that office automation requires a "paperless workflow" and then require typed reports on the progress toward that end, you're sending conflicting messages.

If you tell people that a budget crunch requires them to buy pencils and paper clips with their own money, while the organization's executives are still flying first-class, you're sending conflicting messages.

If you tell people they need to do five new things but don't remove anything from their list of tasks, you're sending conflicting messages. (Telling them to do more with less is simply telling them to cut corners in what may be very dangerous ways. Telling them to work smarter is telling them to do more with less.)

Conflicting messages are confusing in their own right and also provide people with excuses to argue that the new beginning isn't for real.

The second form of reinforcement is a particular kind of consistency: the consistency of your own actions. Regardless of the confusions surrounding a new beginning—and you're sure to have your share—you have one reliable point of leverage in moving people out of the neutral zone: the example of your own behavior.

> *Example is not the main thing in influencing others, it's the only thing.*
>
> Albert Schweitzer, French philosopher

An example used in chapter 2 will illustrate the problem. In that case a promising new beginning was imperiled by a leader who didn't realize how much louder actions speak than words. Anxious to reorganize his people into service teams that integrated formerly separate layers of service techs, the leader ceaselessly preached the benefits of teamwork and collective decision making. But the direct reports on his own staff, each of whom was being told to transform his group into a team, was run dictatorially.

The third form of reinforcement is another kind of consistency. It is common and always disastrous to tell people to act and react in new ways—and then to reward them for the old actions and reactions. You won't manage to hold a new beginning for long

> *It is difficult to get a man to understand something when his salary depends upon his not understanding it.*
>
> Upton Sinclair, American writer

- if you preach teamwork and then reward individual contribution

- if you preach customer service and then reward following the rules

- if you preach risk-taking and then reward no mistakes
- if you preach feedback and then reward no criticism
- if you preach entrepreneurship and then reward "doing your job"
- if you preach decentralized authority and then reward hands-on management.

The rewards in question are not just financial ones. They include all the "strokes" that are given out: time and attention, perks and privileges, praise and awards. People have to feel that they are better off for having changed their attitudes and behavior, and if they don't, you'd better look at your reward system.

Rule Two: Ensure Quick Successes

The neutral zone takes a heavy toll on most people's self-confidence because it is a period of lowered productivity and diminished feelings of competence. It may also, through resonance, uncover serious problems of low self-esteem. For that reason people are likely to need some fairly quick successes if they are to return to their former effectiveness.

These successes can come from small tasks, which can be accomplished even in spite of the damaged self-confidence of transition survivors. They can come from sure wins, situations with little risk of failure. They can even come from ongoing efforts where success was pretty well in the bag before people took them over.

A benefit of quick successes is that when changes are deep and far reaching, new beginnings take a long time to be fully realized. Believers may begin to doubt, and doubters turn into critics. Critics will have a field day. Quick successes reassure the believers, convince the doubters, and confound the critics.

Rule Three: Symbolize the New Identity

People are not merely logical beings; they are full of feeling too. They are not just literal-minded; they also react symbolically to events. That is why apparently small things can take on enormous importance as individuals and their organization struggle to make new beginnings work. Two recent mergers provide examples of this.

In the first case, a serious conflict arose over whether identification badges would be blue (the larger company) or white (the smaller but more successful company). It was decided to make them gold to mirror the new identity. The result: no more conflict and a successful merger. In the second case, one organization was combining with another, and the same conflict erupted over parking stickers. This time it wasn't a true merger: the upper management of the first company was going to run the combined show, and only the supervisors and lower-level employees of the second company were coming aboard. In this case the decision was to adapt the old parking sticker of the acquiring organization with a slightly different type face.

The point is not that such symbolism contributes to success, but simply that it conveys a message that reinforces the new identity being established in the new organizational beginning. During highly charged times of transition, everything takes on a symbolic hue—everything means something. That can trip you up because you don't intend to mean something with everything you do. At the same time, you can use it to your advantage by viewing everything symbolically and looking for opportunities to symbolize the new beginning you are trying to make.

Rule Four: Celebrate the Success

Finally, take time to celebrate arriving in the Promised Land. Just as you marked the endings at the start of transition, you need to mark the beginning at the finish of transition. The timing may seem a little arbitrary because there are always loose ends to be tied up. But when you feel that the majority of your people are emerging from the wilderness and that a new purpose, a new system, and a new sense of identity have been established, you'll do well to take time to celebrate that the transition is over. It may be something as small as a get-together on Friday afternoon or something as big as a victory trip to Acapulco with spouses. In either case, it should be fun and a break from the routine.

It's not a bad idea to let people take away something from this celebration too, a memento of the transition process that is now behind them. The idea is not unlike giving people a piece of the past mentioned in chapter 3. In this case it may be a T-shirt with "I Survived the Merger" across the front or a certificate of thanks for their participation in the transition monitoring team. Serious or a joke, it further acknowledges and ends a difficult time in the organization's history and the person's career.

Conclusion

Behind all of these tactics is the basic idea with which we began, an idea that is more important than any of the tactics themselves: things *start* when the plan says they will, but the *new beginning* takes place much more slowly. If transition is mishandled or overlooked completely, beginnings sometimes fail to take place. Then we say that "the change didn't work" or that it "fell short of our expectations." What we ought to say is that we got the people out of Egypt, but they're still wandering somewhere in the wilderness.

Managing the New Beginning: A Checklist

Yes　No

——　——　Am I distinguishing in my own mind and in my expectations of others between the start, which can happen on a planned schedule, and the beginning, which will not?

——　——　Do I accept the fact that people are going to be ambivalent toward the beginning I am trying to bring about?

——　——　Have I taken care of the ending(s) and the neutral zone, or am I trying to make a beginning happen before it possibly can?

——　——　Have I clarified and communicated the purpose of (the idea behind) the change?

——　——　Have I created an effective picture of the change and found ways to communicate it effectively?

——　——　Have I created a plan for bringing people through the three phases of transition—and distinguished it in my own mind from the change management plan?

——　——　Have I helped people to discover as soon as possible the part that they will play in the new system—or how the new system will affect the part they play within the organization?

——　——　Have I ensured that everyone has a part to play in the transition management process and that they understand that part?

——　——　Have I checked to see that policies, procedures, and priorities are consistent with the new beginning I am trying to make so that inconsistencies aren't sending a mixed message?

—— ——   Am I watching my own actions carefully to be sure that I am effectively modeling the attitudes and behaviors I am asking others to develop?

—— ——   Have I found ways, financial and nonfinancial, to reward people for becoming the new people I am calling upon them to become?

—— ——   Have I built into my plans some occasions for quick success to help people rebuild their self-confidence and to build the image of the transition as successful?

—— ——   Have I found ways to celebrate the new beginning and the conclusion of the time of transition?

—— ——   Have I found ways to symbolize the new identity—organizational and personal—that is emerging from this period of transition?

—— ——   Have I given people a piece of the transition to keep as a reminder of the difficult and rewarding journey we all took together?

Final Questions

What actions could you take to help people deal more successfully with the new beginnings they must make if your change effort is to succeed? What could you do today to get started on this aspect of transition management? (Write yourself a memo below.)[4]

---

[1] Some are ready to, and if they happen to be the organization's leaders, they are unlikely to realize that other people do not respond to ideas as viscerally as they do. They may put out the idea and then wonder why people are holding back. They need to see that ideas alone only galvanize idea-minded people. Others need one or more of the other three P's: pictures, plans, and a part to play.

[2] As I use the term, "picture" has a lot in common with what today is called an organizational "vision." But I use "picture" because "vision" has become associated with "visionary" and is often used in an almost mystical way to refer to something that has the power to revitalize an organization and to realign its people. I don't buy that. Too many visions are pure fantasy that simply alienate leaders from their more down-to-earth followers. Just as relatively few people can be swept up and moved to action by an idea alone, so it is with a vision alone. In the typological categories created by Carl Jung, *thinking* types can be activated by an idea and *intuitive* types can be activated by a vision. But *sensate* types need a plan, and *feeling* types need everyone to have a part in the undertaking.

[3] See the next chapter for specific ways to deal with continuous change.

[4] Note that you may not be far enough into the process of transition to find many of these tactics timely. Just record any that are and use the rest as a checklist for future action. Build them into your transition management plan.

PART THREE

Dealing with Nonstop Change in the Organization and Your Life

Chapter 6

How to Deal with Nonstop Change

There is one fault that I must find
With the twentieth century,
And I'll put it in a couple of words:
Too adventury.
What I'd like would be some nice dull monotony,
If anyone's gotony.

— Ogden Nash, American poet

It must be admitted that there is a degree of instability which is inconsistent
with civilization. But on the whole the great ages have been unstable ages.

— Alfred North Whitehead

It has become a truism that the only constant is change. The Greek philosopher Heraclitus commented on it 2500 years ago. Yet we all feel that change is different today. There's more of it. Our department is reorganized, and that's hardly finished when the new director arrives and decides to reorganize it again. Or just as everyone is recovering from the introduction of the new electronic mail system, they announce that the sales force will start carrying laptop computers and enter orders automatically from the field. We talk not of *a* change but of change as an ongoing phenomenon. It is a collage, not a single image: one change overlaps with another, and it's all change from margin to margin.

That being so, what I've been saying about transition may seem a little artificial—like a pure substance isolated in the laboratory which is never found in nature. In a sense, that's true. The image of transition I've been drawing is an ideal one, like textbook diagrams that are clearer than anything you ever encounter in the real world.

But that clarity has an advantage. Ironically one of the reasons we've paid so little attention to transition is that we're overwhelmed with it. Transition is all around us—so close that we can't see it clearly. Not until we isolate it in its simplest form can we see its outlines. The pure and simple transitions I have been discussing enable people to understand the dynamics of transition more easily than would otherwise be the case. Fortunately, real transitions (like real daisies, real amoebas, and real bullfinches) look enough like their diagrammed counterparts to be recognizable. That said, we now have to adapt the image of the isolated transition to the facts of a constantly changing environment.

*He has too many lice
to feel an itch.*

Chinese proverb

The Three Phases

Overlap

In transition there is an ending, then a neutral zone, and only then a new beginning. But those phases are not separate stages with clear boundaries. The three phases of transition are more like curving, slanting strata in any situation. Or we might see them as overlapping in the manner suggested in Figure 1.[1]

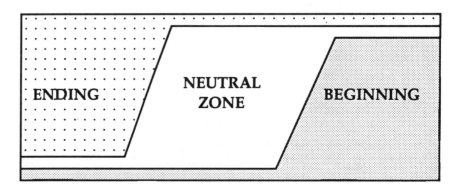

ENDING   **NEUTRAL
ZONE**   **BEGINNING**

Figure 1

In either case, you are in more than one of these phases at the same time, and the movement through transition is marked by a change in the *dominance* of one phase as it gives way to the next.

Add the Fact of Simultaneous Changes

It gets even more complicated. To give an example: in the changeover to a new information management system, you can be almost done (launching the beginning) at the same time you are just entering the transition caused by the recently announced reorganization (letting go of the old structure) and right in the neutral zone after last month's layoffs.

The experience can be compared to conducting an orchestra: you have to keep track of the different instruments, each playing different sequences of notes, some starting and others stopping. While keeping a sense of the whole piece, you have to shift your attention from one section to another. It is important for you to have—or to create—an overarching design to the symphony of change. Without such an overall design, every little change will sound like an unrelated melody that must be started or stopped without regard to the rest of the music.

The first thing you're going to need to handle nonstop organizational change is *an overall design within which the various and separate changes are integrated* as much as possible. In periods of major strategic change, such a design may have been announced to the organization by its leadership. When that happens, you're fortunate. Even if you don't entirely agree with the logic of the larger change, you benefit from the coherence it gives to the component changes.

If, on the other hand, no larger strategy exists, you need to analyze the changes and discover their underlying common purpose. These might include

- the need to save money

- the need to recapture markets lost to a new competitor

- the need to respond creatively to a new climate of public opinion

- the need to speed up decision making by decentralizing authority.

It is sometimes helpful to think of your organization's history as a "life history" and to think of the present as the crossover point between one "chapter" and another. (Imagine what you would entitle those two chapters, and you will have a clearer picture of your change.)

However you do it, you have to find a larger pattern that rationalizes all the specific changes. (A client, recalling the childhood puzzles she liked, recently called it "connecting the dots and discovering the 'hidden object.'") When you've done that, you can use it to orchestrate your responses.

Omnia uno tempore agenda. [Everything had to be done at once.]

Julius Caesar describing how he handled an unexpected, simultaneous attack by the Nervii at three different points on his flanks, while part of his troops were crossing a river and another part were setting up camp

The Rising Tide of Change

You have one characteristic of human nature on your side, though it always seems to kick in too late to make any particular change easy. That is the capacity, over time, to adjust to new and higher levels of change. If a group of eighteenth-century Europeans were transplanted to Silicon Valley or Wall Street, they would be overwhelmed by the pace of change. But each generation is able to assimilate a little more change than the last.

It's changes in *the level or rate of change* that throw us into transition. We talk sometimes as though change was not a problem in the past, but of course it was. A century ago Americans wrote about how fast things were changing and how hard it was to keep up. The rate of change has peaked in the past several decades, and we are having trouble assimilating.

Even if change ceased today, people would have difficulty because the lack of change would itself be a change. The slowing of change is sometimes very disruptive in a young startup company that gets to the point where it must slow down and get some standardized policies and systems in place. Many of the people who were happy with the old chaotic status quo become very unhappy with the new situation. They say things like, "The fun is gone," "This used to be a good company to work for," "We've turned into just another conventional company." (They might, if they were following the suggestion I made earlier, entitle the chapter that was ending, "Goodbye to Camelot" and the new chapter, "Welcome to the Conventional World.")

He who sleeps in continual noise is wakened by silence.

W. D. Howells, American writer

Postpone "Extra" Changes

You can't keep the external world from affecting your organization, but you can often postpone or sometimes cancel incidental changes that are unrelated to the larger shift you're dealing with. The gains from those changes will seldom be large enough to compensate for their disruptive effects, and a crucial large change can be jeopardized by a smaller change that is thoughtlessly piggybacked on the larger one. There is a tendency to think that because we're changing lots of things, we might as well change everything. But that only makes sense if "everything" is an interrelated whole.

The tendency to toss in the extra change also comes about when leaders or managers get personally "hooked" on change. Some people like the adrenalin rush of the crisis situation, and in an environment in which such crises abound, they become habituated to it. (The "new change" also lets them start over whenever the going gets rough, and so saves them from having to do the hard

Two quite opposite qualities equally bias our minds—habit and novelty.

Jean de la Bruyere, French writer

work of implementing that final change.) A change-addicted leader is a dangerous person, although he or she can often be charismatic and can usually make a plausible-sounding case for that next change that is being proposed.

Foresee as Much as You Can

Economic and social forecasting is a big business, but when tested against subsequent events, it misses more boats than it catches. John Naisbitt's *Megatrends*[2] and the megawave of books it launched are fascinating reading, and they address the natural human desire to know what the future holds. The trouble is that they have not managed to forecast events with any degree of accuracy.

Consider the stock pickers. Few of them equal even what you'd achieve with random picks. Or consider the record of the marketeers: The well-researched new Coca-Cola was a fiasco, the much-touted IBM PCjr was a flop, Kodak's disk camera and RCA's videodisk products cost their companies immense sums of money they could ill-afford to lose. Each product was predicted to be a great success by professionals who were supposed to know.

Most predictions are based on the forces that produced today, not those that will produce tomorrow. Those who prepared for "change" in Eastern Europe in 1988 turned out to be ready for 1980, not 1990. They were like the French who built an "impregnable" line of tank-proof fortifications, which they named for their Minister of War, André Maginot—and around which the Germans did an end run in World War II. They were like the companies that embraced the principle of vertical integration, and did so just in time to find that conglomeration was the hot new answer. (By the time they got around to conglomeration, of course, the marketplace favored focus and even niche playing.)

There are two problems with such forecasting. First, everything is so closely interrelated that you can't know enough to say with any confidence what is going to happen. Take something as simple as the price of leather, which has skyrocketed because of a combination of factors that was foreseen by no one: (1) the growing popularity of leather car upholstery by upscale buyers, (2) the growing market for shoes in the People's Republic of China, and (3) the increasing popularity of bomber jackets and other leather clothing. Or consider the unexpected impact on defense spending of the breaching of the Berlin Wall and the sudden thaw in other Warsaw Pact nations. Will new American social programs benefit from the funds released by the defense

Shallow men speak of the past; wise men of the present; and fools of the future.

Marquise du Deffand, French epigrammatist

I have seen the future, and it's a lot like the present, but much longer.

Dan Quisenberry, professional baseball player

cuts, or will the money simply be absorbed by already financially strained, existing programs? The forecasters cannot say.[3]

The second problem is that we aren't the only ones doing the planning, and forecast-based plans create a bandwagon effect that changes the conditions on which the forecasts were based. Walter Macrae made the point very well in an article he wrote for *The Economist* almost twenty years ago:

> In modern conditions of high elasticity of both production and substitution, we will generally create temporary but large surpluses of whatever the majority of decision-influencing people five or ten years earlier believed was going to be in most desperately short supply. This is because the well-advertised views of the decision influencers tend to be believed by both the profit-seeking private producers and consensus-following governments, and these two then combine to cause excessive production of precisely the things that the decision influencers had been saying would be the most obviously needed.[4]

So, because everyone is trying to benefit from the predictions, the predictions prove wrong.

There are, however, two other kinds of forecasting that *can* help you to get ready for change. Neither is so exciting as guessing what numbers will be thrown on the political or economic dice, but both are far more reliable. The first is to do life-cycle forecasts on the organizational policies and structures that you are currently utilizing. Such life-cycle planning is done regularly for products, for everyone knows that sooner or later technological change and competitive pressures will make today's winner an obsolete product. So organizations begin, while the product is still high on the curve of its success, to plan its modification or replacement.

In the same way, life-cycle planning should be done for levels of employment, for areas of technical expertise, or for cultural programs, such as participative management and organizational "excellence." All have as clearly limited a life expectancy as does a product. That retirement package may be almost outmoded, as may the supervisors' training program and the way the organization does its succession planning. Only a life-cycle planning approach to these issues will give you the lead time to avoid the predictable crisis of having to manage the transitions triggered by a change no one expects and few understand. You may not be able to convince people that things that aren't "broke" yet still need fixing, but you can certainly be ready with alternatives when the first cracks are discovered.

Do Worst-Case Scenarios

A second way to be ready for the future is to build into every plan a "what-if?" clause. What if the automation project takes twice as long as everyone says it will? What if 50% more people than you are predicting take you up on the early retirement offer? (And what if they're the wrong people, the ones you want to keep?) What if a government regulation or a legal decision forces you to stop using a certain chemical? What if a 7.2 earthquake hits the manufacturing site or distribution center? What if . . . things don't turn out the way you hope they will?

The only way to prepare for the unexpected is to build into all of your plans a contingency clause that specifies what you will do if the unexpected happens. In that way you will have alternative routes ready for the taking if the main route is closed unexpectedly, and procedures established for aborting your plans with a minimum of chaos if they are undermined by unforeseen events. There is a further advantage to worst-case scenarios: If everyone else, as the Macrae quotation suggests, is going the same way, the worst-case scenario becomes a forecast that may be accurate simply because it is based on the idea that conventional wisdom, which everyone else is using, is likely to be wrong. "Contrarian" investment strategies are based on precisely this assumption.

Make the Transition to "Change as the Norm"

Nonstop change demands a new mindset. That new mindset requires a very significant transition, as the old expectations are painfully abandoned and a long, difficult journey is made through the neutral zone before any viable new beginning is in sight. It isn't enough to preach about the Promised Land by describing the benefits of "continuous improvement" or "thriving on chaos." It isn't even enough to inspire people with vignettes of companies that are said to be doing these things. You have to manage the big transition from the old assumptions and expectations of isolated and piecemeal change to the new ones.

That task is no different from managing any other big transition, and the preceding three chapters should provide the tactics you need. My point is that nonstop change is simply a lot of different changes that overlap each other, and it is an increase in the rate of overlapping change—and changes have always overlapped. Every new level of change will be termed "nonstop" by people who are having trouble with transition.

Stability itself is nothing else than a more sluggish motion.

Michel de Montaigne, French philosopher

At the same time, every previous level of change will be called "stability." Seen in this light, what people today call nonstop change is simply a new level of what has always existed. It isn't pure chaos—simply a new experience. When people adjust to it, it will be a new *stability* of sorts.

These matters are more than simply arguments about the meanings of words. In companies that have successfully institutionalized the practice of "continuous improvement," procedures are constantly being changed to increase production, maximize efficiency, and reduce costs. Little transitions are going on all the time. Without some larger continuity, everyone's world would feel like chaos. But what stays constant is the expectation that every status quo is a temporary expedient until a better way to do things has been discovered. Every one of those little improvements, though it may cause transitions, reaffirms the unchanging values and procedures that underlie continuous improvement.

Not all changes are improvements. Some are small readjustments to maintain the present balance. Some are larger moves to cut losses or to repair damage done by market changes and regulatory actions. The point, however, remains the same: Only if continuous change is normalized as the new status quo can it be assimilated. People have to understand that the point of change is to preserve that which does not change. Endurance depends on change, just as staying upright and traveling straight ahead on a bicycle depends on constant steering adjustments. Refusing to make those little changes would not produce "stability" but would, on the contrary, rapidly lead to the loss of balance and motion.

Clarify Your Mission

Stability through change demands clarity about what you are trying to do. There is no reason to make an adjustment unless there is something to adjust. So a time of continuous change, as exists today, puts a premium on knowing clearly what you are trying to accomplish. What is the mission of whatever it is that you manage—whether it be a small team of hourly workers or a multinational corporation?

The answer to this question is not a matter of high-sounding words, like those company philosophies you see over people's desks. It is a matter of a clear sense in people's minds of how their activities contribute to the entire undertaking. An organization's mission is seldom tricky: General Motors' mission is to build cars and related vehicles, Harvard University's mission is to educate people and push back the boundaries of knowledge, and your community hospital's mission is to provide medical care and treatment that

Progress, far from consisting in change, depends on retentiveness. When change is absolute there remains no being to improve and no direction is set for possible improvement. . . . [W]hen experience is not retained . . . infancy is perpetual.

George Santayana, American philosopher

cannot be given at home or in a doctor's office. Every component part of the larger organization has its own mission, which in some way makes the overall mission possible. Or if it doesn't, you are working with some part that has come unplugged from the whole and whose existence is no longer justified.

Far too many organizational mission statements are really definitions of the organization's objectives: to make a fair return on equity, to produce top-quality products, to be a good place to work. These are important, but they aren't that central, continuous thread that everyday changes are meant to preserve. It is the mission, not the objectives, that is the heartbeat of the organization.

Many are stubborn in pursuit of the path they have chosen, few in pursuit of the goal.

Friedrich Nietzsche, German philosopher

The confusion of missions and objectives has serious repercussions in a time when change is the norm. Sometimes an organization has to make changes in its objectives to preserve its mission:

The company, whose mission is to produce the best possible containers, switches from manufacturing glass bottles to plastic ones.

The company, whose mission is to create high-quality preserved food, shifts from canning to freezing.

The company, whose mission is to provide people with a way to transport packages quickly, sells its rail cars and buys a fleet of airplanes.

Each of these changes can put a corporation into transition, but all of them are undertaken to ensure continuity of mission. The same is true on every organizational level, down to the team level, where people share their more specific collective mission. New machinery is introduced to carry out the mission more effectively. So is the new organizational design or the new policy or the new emphasis on quality or customer service.

The trouble is that people come to identify with the objectives rather than the mission. They do so because it is easier to relate their own efforts and their own self-image to the objective, which is more tangible and closer at hand, than to the mission. But that simply reminds you how constantly you must work to get people to identify with the organization's mission. That takes explanation, modeling, and reward.

Management by objectives works if you know the objectives. Ninety percent of the time you don't.

Peter Drucker, Management expert

Rebuild Trust

If you have ever watched people learning to swim, you've no doubt observed that crucial moment when they push off the edge and free of the teacher's hand and set forth on their own. Without trust in their teacher, it would be impossible. "I won't let you sink," she says. At that moment, with fear balanced against hope, it is trust that makes the difference. Lacking the trust in their own ability to swim, they fall back on trust in their teacher.

It's much the same with transition management. When people trust their manager, they're likely to undertake a change even if it scares them. When they don't feel that trust, progress isn't likely to occur. The good news is that you can build such trust; the bad news is that you can do it only very slowly. It behooves you to get started right away.

There are two sides to trust: the first is outward-looking and grows from one's past experiences with a particular person; the second is inward-looking and comes from one's own history, particularly from childhood experiences. The level of trust any person feels is fed by both of these sources. You have control over the outward-facing one, so start there. The technique is simple— simple to explain, anyway: *start being trustworthy.*

Trustworthiness is encouraged by a number of actions that are within your power to take:

1. Do what you say you will do. Don't make promises you can't or won't keep. Most people's trust problems have been learned from untrustworthy actions in the past.

2. Listen to people carefully and tell them what you think they are saying. If you have it wrong, accept the correction and revise what you say. People trust others whom they believe understand them.

3. Understand what matters to people and work hard to protect whatever is related to that. People trust those who are looking out for their best interests.

If you tell the truth, you don't have to remember anything.

Mark Twain, American writer

4. Share yourself honestly.[5] Hiding shortcomings may improve your image, but it doesn't build trust. Admitting an untrustworthy action is itself a trustworthy action. A lot of mistrust begins when people are unable to read you.

5. Ask for feedback and acknowledge unasked-for feedback on the subject of your own trustworthiness. Regard it as valuable information and reflect on it. It may be biased, and you don't have to swallow it whole. But check it for important half-truths.

He who mistrusts most should be trusted least.

Theognis of Megara, Greek poet

6. Don't try to push others to trust you further than you trust them. Your own mistrust will be communicated subtly and will be returned to you in kind. Trust is mutual or it is very shallow.

7. Try extending your trust of others a little further. Being trusted makes one more trustworthy, and trustworthy people are more trusting.

8. Don't confuse being trustworthy with "being a buddy." Being a buddy for a purpose is an untrustworthy act. Besides, trust doesn't automatically come with friendship.

9. Don't be surprised if your trust-building project is viewed a bit suspiciously. Asking people to let go of their old mistrust of managers and of you in particular means a significant transition. Their mistrust—justified or not—was a form of self-protection, and no one readily gives up self-protection.

10. If all of this is too complicated to remember and you want a single key to the building of trust, just remind yourself, "Tell the truth."

As to what you can do with the inner face of mistrust—which goes back to people's childhood—the same advice holds true. The difference is that if a person's history has reinforced mistrust, you will make even slower headway than combating mistrust you earned by your own actions. But you *can* make headway with even the most mistrustful person, so get started. Every hour that mistrust continues makes transition more difficult to manage than it has to be.

Unload Old Baggage

Managers sometimes find themselves fighting old battles when transition starts. These may even precede the manager's tenure—the layoff back in '73 that was handled so badly; the promise about seniority rights that wasn't kept when the contract was renegotiated; the repeated statements three years ago that the plant wouldn't be closed and it was.

At times like this you feel like yelling, "You're not going to bring *that* up again, are you?" or "You're not blaming *me* for that, are you?" The answer, of course, is "Yes." Transition is like a low-pressure area on the organizational weather map. It attracts all the storms and conflicts in the area, past and present. This is because transition "decompresses" an organization. Many of the barriers that held things in check come down. Old grievances resurface. Old scars start to ache. Old skeletons come tumbling out of closets.

In the short run, this can complicate an already complicated situation. But in the longer run it can have a positive aspect. Every transition is an opportunity to heal the old wounds that have been undermining activity. If leaders have lied in the past, this is the time to tell the truth and to rebuild credibility on the basis of honesty. If people have been dismissed callously in the past, this is the time to terminate people with dignity and fairness and to start building the values of concern and respect for them. If employee concerns have been disregarded in the past, this is a time to begin listening. It is never too late to become an organization that manages its people well. For that reason the old scar and the unresolved issue are great gifts. They represent opportunities for organizational enhancement.

Sell Problems, Not Solutions

As I said in chapter 3, people let go of outlived arrangements and bygone values more readily if they are convinced that there is a serious problem that demands an ending. But the idea of selling problems goes beyond the value of a practical tactic to help manage endings. In an organization in which change is the norm, selling problems is the only way to get beyond having to sell every change piecemeal. Here are some of the reasons that selling problems contributes to your ability to manage nonstop change successfully:

1. People who understand the organization's real problems are in the market for solutions and don't have to be "informed" or "educated" after the fact. When things are changing very fast, often there isn't time to do that.

2. If the manager understands the problem and the people don't, a polarity is immediately set up. If, on the other hand, everyone recognizes the importance of the same problem, it's the manager and people on one side and the problem on the other. Only with such cooperation can organizations respond quickly to the challenges it encounters.

3. If everyone recognizes the problem, it is likely to be solved much faster. Whatever solution is selected is more likely to meet everyone's needs because those needs are clearly stated during the problem solving. Any solution that doesn't take people's needs into account will never sell.

4. Finally, selling problems implicates everyone in the solution. It says, in effect, "If you want to be part of the solution, get involved. If you don't, don't complain."

In light of these points, it is ironic that involving people is sometimes viewed as too time-consuming for a world of rapid change. Actually, the authoritarian style and the command mentality that goes with it take too much time—too much time to slug it out with each pocket of self-interest, too much time to motivate people who feel that the change was forced on them, too much time to argue with people who don't even know that there are problems. Selling problems is, in fact, the investment that pays long-term dividends in making people readier for particular organizational transitions, and for a world of continuous change in general.

The Final Key to Managing Nonstop Change: Challenge and Response

We are constantly hearing about *competitiveness, game plans,* and *winning.* In a society as sports-minded as ours, those terms strike a ready chord—the more so when we seem to be falling behind in a game in which we were once the dominant player. But the sports metaphor is dangerously misleading. It suggests that there is a coherent *game* going on, and that the *winners* will come out ahead because they *beat their opponents.* It suggests that they win because they are a better *team,* with better talent, training, and strategy.

In fact, a world of nonstop change offers only short-term victories to those organizations that set out to beat the opposition. The long-term advantage lies with those organizations that focus on the environment as a whole, not just on the competition. We are in one of those periods of evolutionary shift, and becoming preoccupied with the competition is short-sighted. It is not by competing but by capitalizing on change that today's organizations will survive. This is as true of a department or a project team as it is of organizations as a whole.

The key to capitalizing on change lies in understanding and utilizing the cycle of challenge and response. As historian Arnold J. Toynbee demonstrated in his book *A Study of History*, the great civilizations have risen to power not because of their advantages but because they treated their disadvantages as challenges to which they discovered creative responses.

Toynbee shows, for example, that Athens rose to dominance in the Classical world after its soil was depleted. Instead of being destroyed by that major setback, the Athenians treated it as a challenge to find a new way to participate actively in the economy of their day. Their creative response was to turn to the cultivation of olives, which could draw on much deeper water than could field crops. The Athenians rebuilt their economy around the export of olive oil, which further challenged them to build a merchant marine to transport it, a mining industry to create the coin to pay for goods, and a pottery industry to build the amphoras to contain the oil. New responses thus create new challenges at a lower level of the social organism.

Descending from the serious to the comic, the contemporary television sitcom grew out of the original *I Love Lucy* show, which was itself a response to a challenge that might have doomed a less responsive crew. Lucy and Desi didn't want to live in New York City, where all the TV comedies were filmed and broadcast to relay stations. Instead, they decided to film the show on 35 mm film in Los Angeles and distribute the show like movies through CBS affiliates.

Not only did their response work, but it also changed network distribution patterns and (for better or worse) created the possibility of TV reruns, because the movie film kept its quality much longer than did the then-current kinescopes.

The point of these examples is not that competition is not worth thinking about. It is simply that competition is only of critical importance when the game (to use the favorite competitive metaphor) is not changing very significantly. When a business or industry is going through a profound transformation—and there is hardly one that is not doing so today—competition blinds people to the real challenge, which is *capitalizing on that change*. Competing for market share in today's markets is too much like fighting for deck chairs on the *Titanic*.

The challenge is in the total business environment, internal or external, just as surely as it was once in the natural environment. Some executives see this, as in the case of the airlines executive who recently commented that he wasn't worried about competition from other airlines. His real problem, he said, came from the emerging possibilities of teleconferencing and the potential for reduced business travel. Telecommunications companies, not other airlines, were the real threat. Having identified the real challenge, he needed a creative response.

Challenge and response is the key to success in a time of rapid and far-reaching changes. Most strategic planning is superficial by comparison because it concentrates only on getting a bigger slice of the existing pie—a pie that is not likely to be around much longer.

For the manager there is another advantage to the challenge and response approach to dealing with change: It can be used at any level of the organization. The leadership group faces challenges and comes up with responses, which might be to launch a new product or go after a new kind of customer. Such responses, in turn, challenge upper-level management with their issue: How do we redefine the missions and even the identities of our units in light of this new organizational direction? Their response

challenges middle managers with *their* issue: How do we reorganize our efforts to serve the new unit mission? And their creative responses to that question represents a

challenge to supervisors to come up with new responses at the team level, which in turn

challenges individual workers to respond creatively at the point where the product is made or the service is delivered.

This cascading of challenge and response breaks the stranglehold of passivity that develops when managers, supervisors, and workers see their jobs as merely carrying out the orders of those above them. In a world undergoing nonstop change, every level of the organization must see its situation as a challenge, calling not for compliance but for creative response. When that happens, people are no longer victims who must wait and then act unquestioningly. Challenge and response restores a sense of control and purpose to people, no matter at what level of the organization they work.

Incidentally, it also knocks the socks off the competition, just as it did more than 2,000 years ago in Athens.

Managing in a World of Nonstop Change: A Checklist

Yes   No

____ ____   Have I accepted the fact that nonstop change is the unavoidable reality today, or am I still fighting it?

____ ____   Am I orchestrating my transition management tactics effectively, shifting from change situation to change situation and from an ending here to a beginning there?

____ ____   Do I have an overall design in which this particular transition makes sense?

____ ____   If I do not have such a design, am I working to create one for myself and my people by "connecting the dots" or identifying the "end of a chapter"?

—— —— Am I being careful not to introduce extra, unrelated changes while my people are still struggling to respond to big transitions?

—— —— Am I watching out that I don't stake too much on a forecasted future?

—— —— Am I making (and asking others to make) life-cycle projections to identify and start creating replacements for policies, systems, and structures that have passed their midlife points?

—— —— Do I include worst-case scenarios with my change management plans, both for their own sake and as "contrarian" forecasts?

—— —— Am I planning and managing the transition from "occasional change" to "change as the norm" and encouraging others to do the same?

—— —— Do I honestly think of the status quo as a temporary and expedient resting place in a time of constant change?

—— —— Do I talk of change as the best way to preserve the essential continuity of the organization?

—— —— Have I clarified the mission of my organization and helped others under me to do the same for their level of the organization?

—— —— Are these missions distinguished from our objectives?

—— —— Do I have a deep feeling for this mission, or am I merely mouthing words?

Am I actively working to rebuild trust in the following ways:

—— —— 1. Being very careful to do what I say I will do?

—— —— 2. Listening to people carefully and letting them know what I hear them saying?

—— —— 3. Understanding what matters to people and working hard to protect whatever is related to that?

—— —— 4. Sharing myself honestly (without letting honesty be a cover for hostility)?

—— —— 5. Asking for feedback and acknowledging unasked-for feedback on the subject of my own trustworthiness?

___ ___ 6. Remembering not to push others to trust me further than I trust them?

___ ___ 7. Trying to extend my trust of others a little further?

___ ___ 8. Not confusing being trustworthy with "being a buddy"?

___ ___ 9. Not being surprised if my trust-building project is viewed a bit suspiciously?

___ ___ 10. Constantly reminding myself, "Tell the truth"?

___ ___ Have I worked hard to unpack old baggage, heal old wounds, and finish unfinished business?

___ ___ Do I regularly work to sell the organization's problems?

___ ___ Do I look at my own organizational environment as a challenge and encourage others to do the same?

___ ___ Do I respond to these challenges creatively and help others to do the same—or do we get caught up in competitiveness for a piece of a shrinking pie?

Final Questions

What actions could you take to help people deal more successfully with the nonstop change in which your organization currently finds itself? What could you do today to get started on this task? (Write yourself a memo below.)

---

[1] This way of portraying transition was suggested to me by Donald Skilling, an organizational consultant in Calgary, Alberta, Canada.

[2] John Naisbitt, *Megatrends: Ten New Directions Transforming Our Lives* (New York: Warner Books, 1983).

³ In the months between the writing and the revision of this paragraph, the generally unforeseen war in the Middle East started, and the question of how to use the Peace Dividend became sadly academic.

⁴ Walter Macrae, "The Coming Entrepreneurial Revolution," *The Economist*, 25 Nov. 1976.

⁵ One warning, though: Don't let honesty become a cover and an excuse for hostility. That will destroy trust just as fast as dishonesty will—especially if it isn't honestly expressed.

Chapter 7

Taking Care of Yourself

Streamlined bureaucracies may translate into higher profits, more responsive customer service and faster product development, but they are also forcing difficult adjustments in how managers work. Many managers must adapt to fuzzier lines of authority and greater emphasis on teamwork.

Low-level managers, accustomed to carrying out orders, suddenly are asked to set strategy. For most, a leaner structure means not only increased workloads but also diminished chances for promotion, and the frustration that fosters.

— Carol Hymowitz,[1] American journalist

Life never presents us with anything which may not be looked upon as a fresh starting point, no less than as a termination.

— André Gide, French writer

Never has it been more difficult to be a manager than today. Managers are caught between decision makers, who see no reason their changes can't be up and functioning tomorrow, and employees, who see no reason they have to change what they've done successfully for years. At the same time, the current waves of downsizing mean that managers are stretched thin as they do more with less—less staff, less training, less money, less time to give to critical matters that demand more attention than they can possibly be given. Managers have to delegate responsibility to people who do not inspire a great deal of confidence.

Layoffs and early retirements have removed friends and trusted associates. They have also removed whole layers of management, which once represented the positions into which managers hoped to be promoted. When (and even whether) these managers can look forward to being promoted is uncertain. But even without promotion, they are carrying the responsibilities that once would have brought them higher rank and more pay.

How did I get here?
Somebody pushed me.
Somebody must have
set me off in this
direction . . . for I
would not have picked
this way for the world.

Joseph Heller, American
novelist

Life is like playing a
violin solo in public
and learning the
instrument as one goes
on.

Samuel Butler, English poet

To make matters worse, things aren't easy at home either, and the managers come to work each morning feeling stressed and tired. Family life is full of new situations that their upbringing never prepared them for. Marriages that once would have struggled along unhappily but unchangingly for years break up. Even in intact families, gender roles are changing in confusing ways, as are relations between parents and children. Just as their children seem to be leaving home, their parents need help or even care, and the prospect of freedom disappears under the burden of new responsibility.

The average manager's situation at work and at home is made up of constant and difficult change. It often seems like something between a Greek tragedy and a sitcom. No wonder most managers spend a good deal of time wondering if it is all worth it. And it is understandable if you have been wondering how you'll manage your own transitions. How do you take care of yourself?

That isn't really a self-centered question. In the long run it will be impossible for you to help others effectively if your own situation is deteriorating. You'll either be so distracted that you do a bad job, or you'll unconsciously project your own situation onto others and so misunderstand their needs— and do a bad job. So before you get too far along in managing others, let's see what you should do in your own behalf.

Figure Out What Is Actually Changing

As soon as upper management announces that restructuring, new strategy, or launch of a new product line, you need to figure out how it changes your situation and your future. Be sure that you are seeing the current change in its broadest implications. Here are some examples:

A relatively minor layoff, though it doesn't directly affect you, may mark the end of the no-layoff policy you have always taken for granted.

A new low-priced product line may represent a change in the company's emphasis on top quality and service, which was what made you proud to work for the company.

The closing of a regional office that used to stand between your district office and headquarters may leave you without support services you have always counted on. (The same closing may also flood your district with longer-tenured managers who are looking for a new position—like yours.)

The cutback at the company's research facility may change the company from a technological leader to a "me-too" company. That, in turn, may lead to an exodus of the most talented engineers, who want to be closer to the cutting edge of your field. You could lose critical talent from your team, or good friends, or the mentor who has been helping your career along.

The handsome new headquarters building you're moving into will put you under much closer supervision by your boss, who used to work on the other side of the city. It may also mean a new set of priorities, as money spent to buy an image replaces money spent on equipment and staff.

While you're looking at the big picture, tie it back to the details of everyday reality. Don't stop with generalities like, "I'll be busier" or "We'll have to phase out current operations." Get specific: "I won't have time to get any training this quarter" or "Our design team will probably be reassigned to a new project."

Remember that changes have secondary and tertiary effects, so think about how your own situation could be changed by the indirect fallout from current events. You can't be sure about such things, for unforeseen events could change everything further. But to avoid looking ahead is to say "Forget about that truck heading our way. The driver may notice us in time to swerve."

Decide What Is Really Over for You

What are you going to have to let go of? What's over for you—what are you likely to lose in the transition you face?[2] Those may be hard questions to answer, not only because the effects of change are complex but also because you are likely to react with *denial* when you first face your losses. You're likely, that is, to find it difficult to see clearly and describe accurately the personal ending you face. Perhaps it will help to list some possibilities:

It could be a *dream* that has motivated you thus far in your life and career.

It could be an *assumption* about the rules by which you were playing.

It could be a *tacit understanding* about your value to the organization or the value of the project you care so much about.

It could be the *belief* you have held about your boss or the head of your company—that he or she was ethical, for example, or concerned about his or her employees.

It could even be the *image* you have had of yourself—the faith you had in your competence, honesty, or organizational clout.

An era can be said to end when its basic illusions are exhausted.

Arthur Miller, American dramatist

All of these losses, you will note, are internal ones: feelings, views, understandings, assumptions, self-images. Remember that change deals with the outer situation, whereas transition (and the loss that it triggers) is an internal matter. What you lose is part of yourself.

Loss hurts, so the best clue to loss is pain. What hurts you most in the current change? Spend some time letting yourself experience the feelings. (That may not be easy, for most of us learned to bury those feelings when we didn't know what to do with them.) You may feel bad for somebody else, but push further and ask if the other person's situation means that you're going to have to let go of something yourself. Will you have to give up the idea that you can help your people when they need you? Or that you have to give up the illusion that the same couldn't happen to you? Or that you have to give up a hope of getting ahead while maintaining your self-image as a nice guy?

These are the things you need to mourn. That depression you've been feeling, punctuated with episodes of anger, may be the mourning process you're already undergoing. Recognize the signs of mourning in yourself. As I described them in chapter 3, they were *denial, anger, bargaining, depression,* and *acceptance.* These are not comfortable emotions to have, and you need to avoid acting them out thoughtlessly. Remember that you get to *acceptance* only by getting through the four preceding phases. You can't get around them, and suppressing them is simply going to undermine the letting-go process.

Great is the art of beginning, but greater the art of ending.

Henry Wadsworth Longfellow, American poet

Distinguish Between Current Losses and Old Wounds

Feelings are feelings, and you have to accept them. But some feelings are reactions to the present and some are triggered by the ghosts of past losses that have never been properly dealt with. This relation between the present and unresolved issues from the past is called "resonance" because the current issue activates the past one as one string on a piano or violin can set another vibrating.

Let the past drift away with the water.

Japanese saying

When present situations resonate with painful experiences in the past, they cause far more pain than they otherwise would. Knowledge of this is sometimes all you need because it helps you to feel less frightened. It enables you to say, in effect, "The pain I'm feeling isn't caused by the present situation. That situation isn't as big a threat to me as it feels. It has just touched an old wound." Remind yourself that *that was then, this is now.*

But sometimes even that isn't enough when the pain (whatever its source) is too great. Your past makes you particularly vulnerable to certain kinds of losses in the present. Recognizing the resonance in such a case is valuable because it makes clear that only by working on the old pain and finishing personal unfinished business will you get relief. That is the time most people seek professional help.

Your organization's employee assistance program (EAP) is a good place to start, or consider a pastoral counselor or a psychotherapist. If you have friends who've had a good experience with professional help, ask their advice. Finding someone you're comfortable talking with is more important than which license he or she holds. Testimony from a satisfied customer is your best lead, in these matters as in most others.

Identify Your Continuities

But not everything is ending. A great deal—at work and in the rest of your life—is going to continue. Even in the most radical transitions, it is a piece of your life, not the whole, that is coming to an end. This is a time to take a personal inventory: take stock of the continuities in your life. List them on a piece of paper. Then think of things you've lost track of recently but that used to be a source of continuity in your life: old interests, old relationships, and former recreation you'd like to get back in your life. Add these to your list.

Now think about how to protect or restore these things, these parts of your life that are not threatened by your current losses. What can you do to enhance, strengthen, and reinforce them? Maybe you need to rethink how you're currently spending your time—these continuities may not be getting the share they deserve. You may need to get in touch with someone again or return to a group you've lost touch with. Maybe you need to set clearer boundaries on your obligations to others and create space to take care of your obligations to yourself.

The art of progress is to preserve order amid change and to preserve change amid order.

Alfred North Whitehead

Recognize the Symptoms of the Neutral Zone

Some of the distress you feel is the natural product of being in the neutral zone. No sooner do you begin to come to terms with your losses than you find yourself "lost in the wilderness." When I described in chapter 4 what happens to an organization in this phase of transition, you may have found yourself thinking that you were in that state too—which means that you probably are.

It is a very confusing state. Sometimes you feel empty, dead, flat, inert. You wonder if you'll ever again feel like doing anything that takes effort and motivation. You have to keep going, but your fantasies seem to involve quitting, dropping out, or getting away from it all. At other times it seems like pure chaos. You're surrounded by conflicting signals and contradictory demands. One day things seem to be moving forward; the next day, backward. One day you feel hopeful; the next day there's no hope. Nothing makes sense.

> *I respect faith, but doubt is what gets you an education.*
>
> Wilson Mizner, American humorist

In the neutral zone you may feel you've lost your hold on what everyone blithely calls "reality." Or perhaps it would be truer to say that reality looks very unreal from where you stand. You hear people talking about the everyday things you used to be concerned with, and it sounds strange.

All the time, of course, you must keep doing the necessary things at home and at work. You're busy, even overwhelmed by your life—and, at the same time, feel apart from the world where everyone else acts comfortable and "at home." Occasionally in this state you have moments of clarity in which you suddenly see everything in a new and meaningful light. But then a moment or a day later it is gone. There may be days when you wonder whether you're crazy.

Everyone's experience in the neutral zone is personal to them. Through years of working with people in the neutral zone I've discovered that most of them know so little about this state that they can only conclude that there is something wrong with them. These feelings aren't easy to talk about, so it's easy to assume that they're not "normal." The fact to remember is that they *are* normal.

Take Time-Outs

You probably can't drop out of your life, though the idea sometimes sounds appealing. But you can set off this special time in your life and state you're in. Just as an organization needs to set up special systems and policies for its journey through the wilderness, so do you. You may benefit from making agreements with the people who are closest to you to provide you with a time-out from decisions or from particular responsibilities. You may be relieved to agree that you'll put a hold on special expenses or that you'll do only minimal housework or that you'll give up family get-togethers until things get back to normal. The idea is to decide what temporary arrangements and agreements you must make to get through this time between an old life and a new one.

You will also do well to build yourself quiet times and solid places as a retreat from the chaos of the neutral zone. These may be as simple as a half hour alone in a park, or they may be as involved as a two-week trip to a favorite place in the mountains. Look particularly for islands of stability you can build into your week on a regular basis—times and places you can look forward to when things get crazy.

Another kind of stability you can build in comes in the form of objectives you set yourself and then reach. Most of the time the neutral zone feels end-less, and one day tends to run into another in a manner that makes it hard to know if you're getting anywhere. One way to counter these feelings and to build a kind of structure into the emptiness is to deliberately construct short-range projects. Focus on reaching these goals, and record them as you reach them. It reminds you that things are still getting done.

Use the Neutral Zone as an Opportunity to Take Stock

One way to understand the neutral zone is as a time between one set of purposes in your life and another. So it is not merely a time to take stock of how you're doing in relation to the priorities you have in your life; it is also a time to look at those priorities and to ask if they still make sense to you. The operant term is "to you," for however much these priorities involve others (and they certainly will), they can only make sense in terms of the needs and dreams of one person: you.

No wonder many people recognize that after a big change has taken place in their lives, it was during this neutral zone phase of transition that they suddenly realized they weren't headed where they wanted to be going and that it was time to turn. Sometimes these turns are small course adjust-ments, and sometimes they are big changes in the destination of the personal journey. Whatever they may be for you, this is the time to take stock of where you are headed now and to decide if that is where you want to end up.

Look at Yourself Creatively

When I left college teaching almost twenty years ago and set out to embark on a new career, I found myself caught in a mental trap. When I thought about what I wanted to do, I thought, "Leave teaching." When I thought about what I knew how to do, I thought, "Teach." I knew I couldn't have it both ways—or could I?

The answer turned out to be that the question was wrong because I knew much more than teaching. I knew many of the things that went into teaching: explaining things to people clearly, learning new subjects quickly (sometimes

In this era of world wars, in this atomic age, values have changed. We have learned we are the guests of existence, travelers between two stations. We must discover security within ourselves.

Boris Pasternak, Russian poet

I don't know the key to success, but the key to failure is trying to please everybody.

Bill Cosby, American comedian

Adversity reveals genius, prosperity conceals it.

Horace, Roman poet

a step ahead of the students), working with groups to involve everyone and get tasks done, counseling people who are trying to make decisions, writing logically and effectively, planning learning projects for people (including myself), and organizing my own work schedule. Those were my abilities. "Teaching" was one way of packaging them for use in one particular setting. There must have been many other packages, I decided. And I was right. Writing, speaking, consulting, and training have proved to be four of them.

My ideas about what I'd like to do proved to be as fluid as my abilities. Whenever I had thought about the issue before that time, I had unwittingly assumed that "what I would like to do" meant "where I would like to teach." Not too surprisingly, deciding to leave teaching made me feel I didn't know what I wanted to do. I needed a new way to answer that question. There was, it turned out, no single way, but actually many. I found that things I had enjoyed in the past presented one set of answers, especially if I broadened the inquiry beyond the area of work in the professional sense to include any activity in which I felt productive. I found that things I heard about or read in the newspapers provided another set of answers, although I had to shut off my inner critic, who kept saying, "You couldn't do *that*."

Still other answers emerged in moments of reverie if I took the trouble to note and remember what I was thinking about when my mind drifted. Too often, however, I'd dismiss such daydreaming as wishful thinking.

Then there was the question of resources. I had a professional degree, but it was in the wrong field. I didn't have many contacts in the organizational world. I didn't even have a job. No resources, right? Wrong. I was looking in the wrong place. As a homeowner and as the spouse of a person who was working full-time, I had some very valuable financial resources. I knew people who knew people in the organizational world. And I *did* have a degree (forget the field!). Even my liberal arts training, which seemed so irrelevant to what I planned to do, gave me a storehouse of great quotes.

In short, I did have resources after all. So do you. Resources are simply potential advantages. Some of them are just remodeled disadvantages, things you may have viewed as impediments but which turn out to be the raw materials out of which something interesting can be built.

Finally, there was the question of my own personal temperament. What would be right for me? What was I, by nature? What could I do that went with the grain? I got some help from taking the Myers-Briggs Type Indicator, a widely used scale to determine basic style or nature. It didn't tell me what job to take, but it did give me some important clues about kinds of activities and settings I'd be happiest with. In some ways I was surprised, for once

When I am . . . entirely alone . . . or during the night when I cannot sleep, it is on such occasions that my ideas flow best and most abundantly. Whence and how these come I know not nor can I force them.

Wolfgang Amadeus Mozart,
Austrian composer

again I found that I had a stereotyped view of myself—a picture that didn't square with the facts.

So I found that I badly needed a new view of myself from four different perspectives:

- what I *desired*

- what my real *abilities* were

- what I had in the way of *resources*

- what my *temperament* suggested.

As I've worked with others—many of them managers—whose lives and work situations are changing, I've come back to these four areas again and again. To remember them, I called them DART: Desires, Abilities, Resources, and Temperament.

Life is a series of collisions with the future; it is not a sum of what we have been but what we yearn to be.

José Ortega y Gasset, Spanish philosopher

Consider Your Possibilities in a New Light

This isn't the place to explore all the ways to be creative about your life situation. There are good books on that subject, and I found many of them valuable in my own case.[3] What you will find is that the key to seeing new possibilities in your own life is to break out of the mindset in which everything is just the way it is. That mindset is not in itself a bad thing, for it permits us to get started every morning without having to begin again from scratch. We assume that whatever we were yesterday, we'll be again today and needn't reinvent ourselves every day. But as useful as that decision is, it contains a serious drawback. It keeps us from seeing the thousand other possibilities that exist.

Genius means little more than the faculty of perceiving in an unhabitual way.

William James, American psychologist

The people who break free of yesterday's view of things usually do so in several ways. The first is that they tend to be inquisitive about their own situations, asking "why?" when things seem to be just so and "why not?" when things seem to be impossible. They don't accept the first answers that come to mind because those "answers" usually turn out to be more rationalizations than real explanations. The two simple questions—"why?" and "why not?"—will disclose the possibilities hiding in many apparently solid and unchangeable situations.

A second way in which people can escape from the seeming unchangeability of their lives is to break out of the realm of common sense and consider possibilities that would ordinarily be dismissed as ridiculous or outrageous. Such ideas may not, in themselves, be workable, but they can open the door to others that are. A man who was desperately trying to increase his income to get his family through a hard time while he was starting a business was listing assets he might sell. On a crazy impulse, he wrote down "children." Needless to say, he didn't consider the literal possibility very seriously, but it led him to think of the children as a source of income, which led to the idea of their getting after-school jobs. This proved to be a small but workable part of his solution.

A third way is to look for analogies or metaphors that suggest a new way to see or do something. The inventor of Velcro was trying to think of new ways to stick two surfaces together, when he was pulling burrs out of his dog's coat one day. He got the idea for bonding surfaces with the help of thousands of little hooks. (In an earlier chapter I noted an organizational example of this approach: turning the "sinking ship" metaphor into the "last voyage" as a way of thinking about a factory closure. New possibilities are immediately opened up.)

A fourth way to break out of your everyday view of things is by generating a list of possibilities—15 or 20 of them, ridiculous as well as plausible, trivial as well as serious. When this is done formally in a group, it's called "brainstorming," but you can do it by yourself. Sit down with a piece of paper, write the problem or issue across the top, and write down every solution that comes into your head. Including another person or two in the undertaking will help because their ideas will trigger ideas in you. Don't evaluate the solutions until you're done—don't even worry about whether they're doable. After 10 or 12 ideas you may not have a new course of action, but your old view—that things had to be the way they were—begins to break down.

None of these things is likely, in itself, to give you a fully workable solution to your life and career dilemmas—but that isn't their intent. What they *can* do is to break the roadblock you face most of the time: the view that you simply have no alternatives, or that your only choices are doing what you're doing or being left with nothing.

Experiment a Little Every Day (Starting Today)

You don't have to stop with thinking about these matters. You can act. This probably isn't the time to wager your life and career on one toss of the dice, but it probably is the time to force yourself to do things differently.

Creativeness often consists of merely turning up what is already there. Did you know that right and left shoes were thought up only a little more than a century ago?

Bernice Fitz-Gibbon, American writer

In the beginner's mind there are many possibilities; in the expert's mind there are few.

Shunryu Suzuki, Zen philosopher

- Take a different route to work tomorrow.

- Spend your lunch hour in a totally new way.

- Move your desk.

- Force yourself to pause for a count of three the next time someone asks you a question today, and reply differently from what you'd customarily say.

- Plan to do something this weekend you've never done before.

- Every day this week, force yourself to say "no" to three requests.

- Volunteer to do something you normally wouldn't agree to do.

- Ask somebody that question you've always wanted to ask him or her.

- Next time you're in a restaurant, order something you've never had before.

- Take a three-minute break every hour (or five minutes every two hours) today.

- Every day this week, find at least one occasion when someone is talking about how things have to be a certain way and ask *why*?

- Every day this week, look for a chance to say *why not*? to someone who says that something can't be done.

In short, look for little ways to experiment with new behaviors—starting right now.

Design a Learning Venture

In a time of transition, old knowledge is likely to be outmoded knowledge. You are facing challenges for which your upbringing and education did not prepare you. You are also changing. What used to interest you may not be so interesting these days. You have ideas or hunches that can't be explored without knowing things you don't know today. This isn't the sign that your education was deficient—only that both you and the world have changed and your knowledge and skills haven't yet caught up.

They know enough who know how to learn.

Henry Adams, American historian

Do something about it. Call someone and ask a how-to question. Visit the local library and ask the reference librarian how to find information on an unfamiliar topic. Read a book on a subject you don't know much about. Talk to someone who knows how to do something you'd like to learn, or visit a place where you can watch things being done that you need to learn. Sign up for a course or training program in a new field.

A learning project may involve a formal program at an accredited university, but it need not. Too often people imagine that learning something new will require a great deal of effort and expense. Don't jump to that conclusion until you've explored the issue further. Such an assumption is likely to be one more way you tell yourself, "There's nothing I can do because I don't have the time and money to get totally retrained."

On the other hand, this may be exactly the right time to undertake a long-term educational effort. It doesn't have to lead to a degree, and it needn't be made up of courses in the ordinary sense. It may be your own self-designed combination of reading, weekend extension courses, interviews, and visits. Instead of making excuses, find out what you need to know to explore a possibility or take a next step, and figure out the easiest way to learn it.

Make a Plan to Change Your Life

Our plans miscarry because they have no aim. When a man does not know what harbor he is making for, no wind is the right wind.

Seneca the Younger, Roman statesman

You know about planning—you do it all the time in your work. Establish your goal, then set objectives, then plan backward to identify the steps or stages you will need to move through to get from here to there. You know that you have to identify the resources required and that you have to enlist people who can either help you or who might otherwise stand in your way. You've done this kind of "project planning" a hundred times. The only difference is that this time, *you* are the project.

Remember That Even the Changes You Want to Make Put You into Transition

There *is* a big difference: You have the normal human distaste for transition. You may love change, but losing your old identity and struggling through the wilderness without one is far from a Sunday stroll in the park. The problem of one's own transition undermines many otherwise wonderful plans to do new things in one's life.

Earlier in this chapter I described many ways to deal with your own transition. In earlier chapters I discussed how to help others with endings, neutral zones, and new beginnings, and many of those suggestions can be adapted to helping yourself. (For example, remember the Four P's: purpose, picture, plan, and part to play.) Now is the time to apply all those tactics to your own situation.

A Postscript

Years ago I heard someone mention in an offhand way the four rules she had learned to follow in her life. Although they did not make an impression on me at the time, I jotted them down and have found them growing in importance as the years have passed. They seem particularly important to me during transition, because that is when we find so many of our "rules" outmoded or irrelevant.

Rule One: Show Up

It is startling how often we miss precious opportunities by taking ourselves out of them. All our predictions of success or failure are simply our own imaginings, for we never have a true picture of all the factors in a situation. There is no way to guess how many failures are traceable simply to not giving something a try—to not "showing up" for the event.

Rule Two: Be Present

Some people show up, but they don't give it their best shot. They don't want anyone to say later that they didn't, but they don't bring all of their energies and talents to the table. They merely go through the motions, put in their time.

Rule Three: Tell the Truth

Saying what you think you are expected to say has several drawbacks. First, you may get the expectation wrong. Second, the expectation may suddenly change—in fact, it can be guaranteed to change these days. Third, it is difficult to keep clear on what you've said in the past, especially when expectations keep changing. Fourth, it destroys your mind and spirit. Telling the truth is often the most powerful action you can take. Many seemingly overwhelming problems have been transformed when someone finally told the truth.

Rule Four: Let Go of Outcomes

In this day of heightened accountability, it's tempting not only to do our best but to try to manipulate the system to bring about our desired ends. But we cannot ultimately control outcomes, and when we try to, we either alienate others or drive ourselves crazy. Wisdom through the ages has always counseled a wise relinquishment: Learn to do all that you are able, then let go.

Taking Care of Yourself: A Checklist

Yes   No

____   ____   Have I determined how my situation and my future have been changed by the recent, the current, or the planned organizational changes? What exactly is going to be different for me?

____   ____   What part of myself am I losing or am I likely to lose in the transition that is triggered by my change? Something that has been important to me is ending. What is it? What is it time for me to let go of?

____   ____   What losses in my life outside of work may be amplifying the feelings I'm getting from the endings that are taking place on the job?

____   ____   Can I identify signs of mourning in myself? If so, do I accept them as natural, or am I trying to get over it and move on quickly?

____   ____   Have I tried to separate my reaction to the present from the resonance it may be setting off within me? And if the resonance is strong, have I sought professional counseling?

____   ____   Have I stopped and reflected on the continuities in my life (including those I've temporarily lost touch with) and done whatever I need to do to strengthen them?

____   ____   Am I recognizing many of my feelings as the normal symptoms of life in the neutral zone, or am I imagining that they mean there is something personally wrong with me?

____   ____   Have I made the necessary temporary arrangements and agreements to give myself a temporary time-out from decisions and responsibilities that can wait?

—— —— Have I found quiet times and stable places to give myself a respite from the chaos I so often feel around and within me these days?

—— —— Have I set short-range objectives for myself to restore a sense of movement and achievement during this time?

—— —— Have I taken the time to take stock of where I stand in my life now, both in relation to the goals I have set myself in the past and in terms of my own present dreams and needs, which might make other goals more rewarding to me?

—— —— Am I actively trying to see myself with new eyes, especially in terms of what I desire, my abilities, my resources, and my basic temperament? (Remember DART.)

—— —— Am I pushing myself to break out of my old ways of seeing my life and the options I have today?

—— —— Am I asking *why?* and *why not?* when I look at how my life is at the moment? (And am I not accepting the ordinary, common-sense answers to those questions?)

—— —— Am I letting myself play with outrageous possibilities, viewing them as paths that may lead to something workable in the long run?

—— —— Am I thinking of analogies and metaphors for my situation ("It's like a . . .) and then trying to change them and come up with new ones?

—— —— Have I pushed myself (preferably with others' help) to write down 15 or 20 different things I could do in my present situation?

—— —— Am I committed to experimenting with my life this week?

—— —— Have I designed a learning venture for myself, a way to acquire the knowledge and skills I need to deal successfully with my new opportunities?

—— —— Do I have a "project plan" (as well-thought-out as I'd make for a work project) for what I'm going to do with my life and career at this point?

—— —— Have I taken into account transitions that are likely to occur as I pursue that plan, and have I taken steps to manage them?

Finally, am I remembering the only four rules of living that I'm likely ever to need?

_____ _____   Am I showing up?

_____ _____   Am I being present?

_____ _____   Am I telling the truth?

_____ _____   Am I letting go of outcomes?

Final Questions

What actions could you take to help yourself deal more successfully with the personal and organizational transitions in which you currently find yourself? What could you do today to get started on this task? (Write yourself a memo below.)

---

[1] "When Firms Cut Out Middle Managers," *Wall Street Journal*, 5 April 1990, B1.

[2] The same questions can be asked about changes in your nonwork life. These, too, put you into transition and lead to losses. Often those nonwork losses combine with those at work to add to your load. Sometimes the nonwork losses amplify the feelings caused by the work-related losses—as, for example, when your dreams of a happy marriage come to an end at the same time that your career expectations are being challenged. The two reinforce each other and make the situation much harder to deal with.

[3] Refer to the books cited in chapter 4.

Part IV

The Conclusion

Chapter 8

A Practice Case

The mistakes are all there waiting to be made.

— S. A. Tartakower, Russian chess master, speaking of the chess board at the beginning of a game

Six chapters ago you tried your hand at the case of the software company that wanted to form its individual contributors into service teams. Now I'll present another case to see if you can apply what you've been reading.

You work for Apex Manufacturing, a 4,000-employee firm that used to be the world's foremost company in its field: small, specialized gasoline motors. Together with two domestic competitors, which had been founded by alumni from your company, Apex made most of the world's supply of such motors— in 1980, it alone made 52% of the motors produced.

Since 1980, however, two Asian firms and one German company have entered the field, and one of the American competitors has invested huge amounts of money in new plants and equipment. To make matters more difficult, new governmental noise abatement standards have forced Apex to redesign the motors' exhaust systems. Somehow, your competitors foresaw these new standards and built them into new designs. You didn't, and had to make costly modifications. By the end of the '80s, you had only 43% of the world's market, and that figure was falling.

There have been rumors of impending plant consolidations and staff layoffs for some time, but only a week ago the CEO was quoted in a *Wall Street Journal* article as saying that Apex would be able to do its trimming by attrition alone and that he expected sales figures to increase significantly by the end of the year. "We're just caught in one of those cycles," he said. "We'll have 50% of the world market again within two years."

Yesterday morning you received an Email message from the vice president of personnel asking you to come to a noontime meeting in her office.

When you got there, you saw a dozen of the company's most respected managers—everyone from supervisors to directors. The VP told you briefly that several decisions had been made by the leadership team.

First, two of the company's five plants will be closed, affecting 900 non-exempt workers and 100 exempts, about a third of the company's manufacturing group. The situation will be complicated by several factors. The two plants made one of the company's more modern and successful lines of motors. The locations of the plants raised costs and led to their being pegged for closure. The plants must continue producing motors for at least eight more months while other plants are readied to take over their production.

Second, there is to be a 20% reduction in the level of employment at the company—800 jobs. All departments are to make cuts, though specific targets for different groups have not yet been set. Neither have the provisions of a possible early retirement plan. It has not even been decided how many of the terminated employees will be from among the 1000 extra manufacturing employees. Many of them were long-term employees whom the VP of manufacturing wanted to reassign to one of the other plants or to some other part of the company.

"There are still a lot of questions," the personnel VP said. "But you are being called together as a transition management advisory group. The leadership team made the decision as to *what* will be necessary—downsizing and consolidation. We're asking you to help us work out *how* we should do it. Specifically, you are being asked to come up with a scenario for announcing and implementing the closure and for working out a plan for handling the reductions in the workforce.

"We're going to meet together all day tomorrow," she continued, "and I want you to clear your calendars. We have to get a tentative plan back to the leadership team within ten days. It doesn't have to be detailed, but it does have to sketch out the issues we need to be ready to deal with and give us some ideas for dealing with them. We want it to advise us on communications, training, and any new policies or arrangements we need to have in place to get people through the transition."

Then she handed out a sheet on which she had listed some of her own concerns:

Transition Management Concerns

1. Apex has not had a layoff in the past 20 years. During most of that time it was growing.

2. The 1000 workers from the two plants to be closed include some highly talented people that the organization would hate to lose.

3. There is a strong sentiment among the leadership team for an across-the-board cut in employment levels ("It would be fairer"), but the personnel VP and some others share a concern that some parts of the company are already dangerously lean while others are "fatter."

4. There is a perception among rank-and-file employees that the senior managers, whose pay has always been generous, are not bearing enough of the brunt of the difficulties of the company they led.

5. The basic announcement of the decisions is scheduled to go out tomorrow in a memo to all employees. A copy is attached:

> TO: All Apex Employees
> FROM: R. E. Owens, President and CEO
> REGARDING: Measures Needed to Restore Profitability
>
> In order to recover ground lost to foreign competitors, who have been able to dump their government-subsidized products on the American market, the executive team has decided to consolidate all manufacturing into the plants at Worthington, San Jose, and Little Rock. The plants in Stevens Mills and Grandview will be phased out over the next eight or nine months.
>
> During the same period, employment levels in the company, which have recently risen past the 4000 mark, will be readjusted to a level around 3200. At that level we will be able to maintain profitability if we can contain other costs. In the latter regard, all employees are asked to refrain from ordering supplies and equipment unless it has been personally approved by a member of the senior management team.
>
> Apex has a noble tradition, but in recent years too many of our employees have forgotten that we must make a profit for our stockholders. If, however, we can tighten our belts and do more with less, we'll not only climb back into the black, but we'll also recover the market share that slipped through our fingers when we let ourselves get too comfortable.
>
> I will be back in touch with you when the details of the plant closures and the layoffs have been determined. In the meantime, I am sure that I can count on your continued hard work and loyalty.
>
> R. E. Owens
> President and CEO

"We're in a tight spot," the VP concluded. "Frankly, I'm not sure all the senior managers realize how tight it is. I'm looking to you folks to help me make the case for handling the human side of this whole mess with some care. And I'm looking to you to help me show that there is, in fact, a way to do it that doesn't just drop everything on the people like a bomb and then leave them to take care of their own wounded."

"I'd suggest that you go back to your units and arrange to free up the next couple of days. Then I'd like you to look over the following list of suggestions that were made by different members of the senior management team and rate them on a scale of one to five."

We'll compare reactions in the morning and come up with some first steps."

You go back to your office, get the secretary to postpone and cancel your meetings and start to work on the list of suggestions. (*Do that now. Write a number to the left of each item on the list. Finish doing so before you continue.*)

1 = Very important. Do this at once.

2 = Worth doing, but takes more time. Start planning it.

3 = Yes and no. Depends on how it's done.

4 = Not very important. May even be a waste of effort.

5 = No! Don't do this.

____   Cancel the memo and don't distribute any communications until firm plans have been made for the details of the layoffs and plant closures.

____   Rewrite the memo to convey more sensitivity to the impact on the company's employees.

____   Set up a "manufacturing restructuring task force" to recommend the best way to consolidate operations and how to determine the disposition of the 1000 excess workers from the plants at Stevens Mills and Grandview.

____   Set up a "downsizing suggestion plan" through which everyone can have input into how the downsizing will be carried out.

____   Sell the problem that forced the changes.

____   Fire the CEO.

____   Bring in all site managers and directors for an extensive briefing. Hold a no-holds-barred question-and-answer session. Don't let them leave until they're all satisfied that there is no better way to handle the situation.

_____ Make a video explaining the problem and the response to it. Hold all-hands meetings at each company site, where the site manager takes and answers all questions.

_____ Set up a hot line to give employees current, reliable information.

_____ Get the senior management team to agree to a one-year 20% cut in their own salaries.

_____ Order an across-the-board 20% budget cut throughout the company.

_____ Institute a program of rewards for cost-saving suggestions from employees.

_____ Plan closure ceremonies for the two plants.

_____ Use the time the company spends in the neutral zone to redesign the whole business: strategy, employment, policies, and structure.

_____ Get the CEO to make a public statement acknowledging the tardiness of the company's response to the realities of the marketplace.

_____ Make it clear up front that the company is headed into a protracted period of change.

_____ Explain the purpose, picture, plan and the parts people will be playing in the announced changes.

_____ Circulate an upbeat news release saying that this plan has been in the works for two years, that it isn't a sign of weakness, that its payoff will occur within a year, and so on. In all communications, accentuate the positive.

_____ Allay fears by assuring workers that the two plant closures are the only big changes that will take place.

_____ Develop or find career-planning seminars to help people whose jobs are being threatened or lost because of the changes.

_____ Immediately set new, higher production targets for the next quarter so people have something clear to shoot for and so that by aiming high, they will ensure adequate output even if they fail to reach the goals.

_____ Make a video in which the CEO gives a fiery "we gotta get lean and mean" speech.

_____ Analyze who stands to lose what in the changes.

_____ Redo the compensation structure to reward compliance with the new system.

_____ Help the CEO put together a statement about organizational transition and what it does to an organization. The result should be empathetic and concerned about people.

_____ Set up transition monitoring teams in the Stevens Mills and Grandview plants, as well as in other units that are significantly affected by the changes.

_____ Appoint a "change manager" to be responsible for seeing that the changes go smoothly.

_____ Give everyone at Apex a "We're Number One!" badge.

_____ Put all managers through a quality improvement seminar.

_____ Reorganize the leadership team and redefine the CEO's job as a team coordinator.

_____ Give all managers a two-hour seminar on the emotional impacts of change.

_____ Plan some all-hands social events in each company location—picnics, outings, dinners.

_____ Launch a plan to buy the smallest of Apex's domestic competitors to gain market share and a strong research and development group.

_____ Find ways to "normalize" the neutral zone and to redefine it in terms that have more benefit to both the organization and its employees.

As in chapter 2, the following comments are not meant as "right" answers, but as advice that has proved to be generally useful in such cases.

Category 1: Very important. Do this at once.

Rewrite the memo to convey more sensitivity to the impact on the company's employees.

The current memo is a disaster. (Memos themselves are not the best way to convey information like this if an all-hands meeting is possible, though in a multisite organization it isn't.) The tone of the memo disowns any leadership responsibility for the situation and leaves the impression that people haven't worked hard enough. See the following items for ways in which the public announcement could be improved, but at the head of the list needs to be "more sensitivity to the impact on the company's employees"!

Get the CEO to make a public statement acknowledging the tardiness of the company's response to the realities of the marketplace.

Whatever the CEO says, his credibility has already been compromised. Just a week ago he was telling a *Wall Street Journal* reporter that everything was going to be great. It's very important to address this credibility problem directly and quickly—and to take responsibility for past mistakes.

Make it clear up front that the company is headed into a protracted period of change.

This is the next step in the program of credibility-rebuilding. It is tempting to be "reassuring" and even to cut a few corners in an attempt to be. But that is very dangerous because the reassurance lasts only a little while, and what lasts a long time is the mistrust generated by false reassurances.

Sell the problem that forced the changes.

To do this, you'll first have to "sell the problem" of transition-related problems to the CEO. Until he buys the problem, he isn't going to buy the solution—which is talking publicly about the organization's real problems. But until he's ready to do this, he won't be able to sell any of his planned changes as the best way out of the company's difficult situation.

Help the CEO put together a statement about organizational transition and what it does to an organization. The result should be empathetic and concerned about people.

This depends, of course, on the CEO's *understanding* organizational transition. You may need to administer a little shock therapy to get the message across, and this will probably have to come from an outsider. In an organization that has hidden its head in the sand as long as this one has, it's hard for inner alarms to be heard. Assuming that you can get the CEO to understand the transition-related problems, his open discussion of them will set the tone for the whole transition management effort that is going to be necessary if the current changes are not to start the company sliding down the slope to disaster.

Bring in all site managers and directors for an extensive briefing. Hold a no-holds-barred question-and-answer session. Don't let them leave until they're all satisfied that there is no better way to handle the situation.

These men and women are going to have to answer a thousand questions from their people. They will have to feel the rightness of the actions in their bones. If they believe in what is being done, they will bring others along with them. If they don't, everyone is in trouble. Get this group on board immediately. Tell them the truth—even if some of it has to be withheld from others for the time being—and give them the chance to ask any and all questions. Don't pull punches with this group, and don't delay talking with them.

Make a video explaining the problem and the response to it. Hold all-hands meetings at each company site, where the site manager takes and answers all questions.

Perhaps this belongs in Category 2, because it obviously takes a little time—although if it's a simple video of the CEO (and perhaps others in the leadership group) talking about the problems and their solutions to them, it can be put together pretty quickly. The video is part of the communications effort to get beyond memos and present at least the semblance of the leadership's personal communication. (It may work better for the leaders to make a rapid flying tour of the company's various locations.)

Appoint a "change manager" to be responsible for seeing that the changes go smoothly.

Even before the details of the changes are clear, it is certain that they will involve things that span different areas of authority and fall in no one's area of authority. Someone must oversee these things—the regular lines of authority aren't adequate. The person appointed can be someone with another position who is also given this job; this works only if there is some way to relieve the person from conflicting duties. Or it can be someone who is taken out of his or her regular job completely and made the change manager for the duration of the changes. Realize, though, that this person acts as an overseer or a coordinator, not a boss.

Set up transition monitoring teams in the Stevens Mills and Grandview plants, as well as in other units that are significantly affected by the changes.

The leaders need new channels of upward communication and need them immediately. The TMT is the easiest way to achieve this. Don't sit passively and listen. Engage the TMT in a dialogue, try ideas on them, ask for their advice, argue (nonbelligerently) with them—and then act on what they tell you. If you don't act, the TMT will quickly be tagged as just another management scam.

Category 2: Worth doing, but takes more time. Start planning it.

Explain the purpose, picture, plan and the parts people will be playing in the announced changes.

This is the heart of transition management, but it is impossible to do it up front. You can talk about the purpose (the *why* of the changes), but only the sketchiest kind of picture of the organization is going to come out of the changes. And the plan is only a plan for a couple of first steps. The Four P's are the planning group's agenda, but they are going to take months to work out in the detail necessary for their success. Besides, management first needs to concern itself with endings and neutral zone issues.

Analyze who stands to lose what in the changes.

This is a critical task but one that takes time. Nor is it a one-time task, but rather an ongoing habit for people to develop as they plan and implement the thousands of changes that will be part of the big plan. (You might consider starting with what the CEO stands to lose by acknowledging that the response to the new market conditions has been dangerously tardy. Such losses may well stand in the way of his playing an effective leadership role, unless you can think of ways to help him let go.)

Give all managers a two-hour seminar on the emotional impacts of change.

Determining who's going to lose what is just the first of many transition management tactics with which managers must become familiar. A short seminar, held as soon as possible, may be the best way to help people recognize that they have indeed lost something in these changes, that "grieving" is normal and usually involves emotions like *anger* and *depression*, which are easily mistaken for "bad morale" and may even be punished.

Set up a hot line to give employees current, reliable information.

You might put this in Category 1 because it is very important to provide fast, accurate, and reliable sources of information. But don't set up a hot line until you've created reliable machinery to have it answered, to process the questions that it generates, and to return the answers to the questioners. Any communications medium that raises more questions than it answers is dangerous.

Set up a "manufacturing restructuring task force" to recommend the best way to consolidate operations and how to determine the disposition of the 1000 excess workers from the plants at Stevens Mills and Grandview.

What faces Apex is not simply a task of closing down a couple of plants or laying off 800 excess workers. The danger is that those changes, so formidable in themselves, will preoccupy people to the point that they forget that these things were necessary because an organization had allowed itself to maintain a status quo which was daily growing more obsolete. If Apex is to be revitalized, its manufacturing must be redesigned. That is the mega-change, and it needs to be designed by the people who have to make it work. Hence the task force, made up of a combination of the brightest critics within manufacturing and representatives of the group that now holds power. They will also need outside expertise, but no experts can do the job for them.

Develop or find career-planning seminars to help people whose jobs are being threatened or lost because of the changes.

The 1000 people displaced by the plant closures have just run into a solid wall in their career paths. They need help in rethinking their careers. So do the people who will be displaced in the larger company reorganization that will surely take place. If you provide them with career assistance, those who leave the company will take with them a positive feeling about the organization because it helped them to find work elsewhere, and those who stay will be grateful for the assistance in redirecting their efforts inside Apex. Lacking such help, the "leavers" will be angry and will talk down the company at every chance, and the "stayers," bitter and frustrated, will undermine the company's ongoing operations.

Plan closure ceremonies for the two plants.

These places have been a home and world to many people. They need a way to disengage themselves from that world. Some organizations hold funerals, some hold wakes, and some create unique ceremonies of closure. The details of what is done are far less important than is the fact that representatives of the affected groups themselves do the planning and implementation. It has to be *their* event. The planning takes a great deal of time and is itself a therapeutic process. Start right away.

Institute a program of rewards for cost-saving suggestions from employees.

What is happening at Apex is much more than simple cost-cutting, but saving money is an important part of the solution to the company's problems. Soliciting suggestions from employees is an important action. Not only does it draw on an often untapped expertise, but it also challenges people to be conscious of the costs of what they do. It also engages them in the search for a solution, rather than forcing a solution on them. (Be sure to give them a slice of the savings, though. They're sharing the pain; they ought to share the gain.)

Find ways to "normalize" the neutral zone and to redefine it in terms that have more benefit to both the organization and its employees.

Take care of endings first, of course, but begin thinking about what is sure to be a long time in the wilderness. The journey from what Apex used to be to what Apex needs to become is probably going to last for several years. Like any confusing and ill-defined time, people are likely to project their fears onto it. You need to help them to understand why they are so uncomfortable during this time. You must find a more meaningful metaphor for it. Remember the "sinking ship" and the "final voyage of the ship." The latter gave people a context in which they can help themselves and the organization. The former, which simply expressed everyone's fears, did not.

Use the time the company spends in the neutral zone to redesign the whole business: strategy, employment, policies, and structure.

This is the opportunity that is embedded in the dangerous situation in which Apex now finds itself. This is the chance—and in today's situation, probably the last chance Apex will get—to transform the company from yesterday's industry leader (and today's critical case) into tomorrow's comeback champion. Everyone's attention has been caught. The debates over the need to change have stilled. This is the time to seize the initiative and convert a necessary reorganization into a complete revitalization. This will take a long time, but must be begun immediately. Only out of such a complete redesign effort can a convincing new picture of the organization emerge. Without such a picture, it's just pushing players around on the board with no strategy and no clear plan.

Category 3: Yes and no. Depends on how it's done.

Order an across-the-board 20% budget cut throughout the company.

That's a huge cut, and if you simply order that it be made, the results are likely to be disastrous. A totally redesigned organization might well be able to turn out its present output or more for one-fifth less money. But you cannot take the old organization, lop off a fifth of its resources, and tell it to keep on turning out the widgets at the old rate. Still, as a target figure, 20% is important. The divisions can use it as a guideline to generate savings of, say, 10%. The remaining 10% will probably have to come from discontinuing unproductive operations or having costly support services be provided by outside vendors.

Get the leadership team to agree to a one-year 20% cut in their own salaries.

This has more merit. It is the kind of step that would seize people's imaginations and send a clear message that the leadership was serious. The trouble is that if it is done by fiat, it will generate hostility from the very people who have to lead the new charge on the opposition, so it can't be imposed. Senior managers must be made to understand the problem and the need for a powerful attention-getting symbolic action. They may need new evidence that what people believe to be their unfairly high pay is undermining their credibility. The problem is that there may be no one within the group who will champion this message. Everyone's immediate self-interest may get in the way of their long-term self-interest, which is to revitalize the company. This is one of the many areas in which an outsider may be useful.

Plan some all-hands social events in each company location—picnics, outings, dinners.

In the neutral zone such events can help to protect or to rebuild the solidarity that has been damaged by losses and the confusion people feel. But they have to be timed effectively. Done at the wrong time, they take on a "bread and circuses" quality, like the giveaways and the spectaculars that the late Roman emperors used to keep their restless subjects distracted and quiet. So deal with endings first, then consider such events.

Make a video in which the CEO gives a fiery "we gotta get lean and mean" speech.

Several things about this are wrong. First, the CEO hasn't yet done anything to restore his credibility—such as leveling with people or taking a 20% pay cut. Second, this isn't a time for organizational weight loss; instead, the whole organization needs to be redesigned. Third, "lean and mean" is a cliché that has lost much of its power to move people. To the extent that tightening and trimming are the answers, the need for them has to be communicated in a fresh and believable way.

Set up a "downsizing suggestion plan" through which everyone can have input into how the downsizing will be carried out.

We've already established that employee suggestions have many benefits and ought to be solicited—particularly on how to save money in the everyday conduct of business. There will also be a time for employee input into the redesign process. But to throw something as difficult and painful as layoffs open to "employee suggestions" is to court disaster. One way to involve employees in the process is to set up an employee group to advise management on selection criteria for deciding who should be terminated. The process may be no better than the one management would come up with itself, but involvement leads to buy-in. And management doesn't need any more processes that employees refuse to buy into.

Fire the CEO.

This has appeal. The guy sounds like a jerk. Maybe he lacks the wherewithal to get people through the next few years. But watch out. Companies often get the leadership they deserve, and to punish the leader for failures that were the product of many minds is just scapegoating. It's unfair, and it doesn't do any good. It may even strengthen the refusal of the CEO's loyal troops (and they are probably many) to go along with whatever redesign effort is undertaken by a new leader. Beyond these considerations, a change in leadership at this time will bring a whole new army of changes into the field. Be sure that the gains exceed the costs. (All this said, it is unlikely that this CEO will last more than a couple of years regardless of what you do. He is too tarred with the brush of failure to be able to lead a revitalized organization.)

Category 4: Not very important. May even be a waste of effort.

Launch a plan to buy the smallest of Apex's domestic competitors to gain market share and a strong research and development group.

At crisis points organizations sometimes turn outward to solve what are really internal problems. It's like the married couple who decide to have a new baby to save their marriage. The results are likely to be disastrous—not only because the solution doesn't solve anything, but also because the solution further burdens an already overburdened system. Yet the impulse to acquire what the company does not have is not all wrong. If it were part of the larger redesign, it might be a great move. But now it's not, so forget it.

Reorganize the leadership team and redefine the CEO's job as a team coordinator.

Again, the impulse may have some merit. Apex is an old-line company, and its governance system is probably outmoded. (Certainly it hasn't been making wise decisions lately.) *If* the redesign we have been discussing created a different kind of structure that demanded a different kind of governance, and *if* a more egalitarian culture emphasizing teamwork proves to characterize the new organization, then a leadership team run by a coordinator-CEO would make sense. But those are big "ifs." As an isolated change, it will just deepen the mess everyone is in.

Put all managers through a quality improvement seminar.

Quality may indeed be an area in which Apex is losing ground to its competitors. But a quality improvement program is a major undertaking, one that generates a whole field of individual and group transitions. To overlay that on the reorganization that is now under way is asking for trouble. At a later point, when the picture is clearer, quality improvement may prove to be a critical piece of the outcome Apex is seeking. Until then it's a 500-pound sack that you're going to load onto the back of an already overloaded camel.

Redo the compensation structure to reward compliance with the new system.

Maybe this, too, will prove to be a good idea somewhere down the line, after the Four P's are clearer. But for now, no new roles, attitudes, or behavior can be said unequivocally to deserve special reward. (The one exception is the bonus that should be paid for valuable suggestions.)

Category 5: No! Don't do this.

Cancel the memo and don't distribute any communications until firm plans have been made for the details of the layoffs and plant closures.

This is guaranteed to turn confusion into total chaos. People know that something big is up. A pirated version of the CEO's unfortunate memo is likely to be faxing its way from site to site and office to office. The secretaries had the news before the VPs, so don't imagine that you can put a cap on this story. Instead, move forward with all the speed you can. Tell people what is afoot and then tell them when they can expect to hear the next installment. If that deadline proves unworkable, tell them why and then tell them when they can expect the next communication. Don't let communications cease. People abhor a communications vacuum. Besides, the local business reporters are already at work on a story that will tell people more than you were planning to. So seize the communications initiative. Start talking.

Allay fears by assuring workers that the two plant closures are the only big changes that will take place.

You can't say this! It's almost certain to be untrue. It will be perceived as one more of management's lies and another good reason "not to believe a damned thing they say." It's far better to say that these are the only changes that have been decided on at present but that further changes will undoubtedly have to be made and that people will learn of them as soon as they have been decided on.

Immediately set new, higher production targets for the next quarter so people have something clear to shoot for and so that by aiming high, they will ensure adequate output even if they fail to reach the goals.

These tactics are getting worse and worse. It's almost certain that output is going to fall, at least temporarily. When that happens, people who already feel inadequate will have evidence that their feelings are right. Far better to set lower targets and exceed them than to achieve slightly higher productivity and a lasting sense of failure.

Circulate an upbeat news release saying that this plan has been in the works for two years, that it isn't a sign of weakness, that its payoff will occur within a year, and so on. In all communications, accentuate the positive.

"Be positive!" is one of those dangerous half-truths that are constantly snagging us on the false half. It's important for people to be led by others who believe and say "we can make it," but it's very dangerous to leave the impression that the path will be easy or that the outcome is certain. Far too much positiveness consists in leaving that impression. Realism is increasingly important as people get further into the redesign process. By that time they can see what they're up against. And "positive thinking" is likely to sound more and more like "wishful thinking."

Give everyone at Apex a "We're Number One!" badge.

Apex can barely stay afloat! Somebody has been watching too many basketball playoff games. This is the worst kind of positive thinking—not to mention being irrelevant. Not a good combination. Mottos are useful, but only when they effectively capture a real emerging possibility. When they are just words, they simply reinforce what is probably already too prevalent an opinion: This company's being led by a bunch of jerks!

Well, how did you do? Better than in chapter 2, I bet. In categorizing these options, I found myself debating which rating to give several of them, and if I did it again I might do it differently. The idea is not to put all the items in the same categories that I did but to make decisions *with people in mind.*

Whatever plans the leadership at Apex (or you yourself) come up with are going to represent changes in the world that people have known. Such changes create transitions, and transitions have to take place if the changes are to work. The odds of transitions actually taking place as planned will rise greatly if you make your decisions with the basic transition-management tactics in mind.

Chapter 9

Conclusion

A great war leaves a country with three armies: an army of cripples, an army of mourners, and an army of thieves.

— German proverb

This proverb comes from centuries of experience with the traumatic changes that accompany conquest, and it deserves at least a footnote in any organizational plan for strategic change. It reminds us that whatever conquerors gain, they leave behind three groups of survivors: those who have been wounded in the process of change, those who grieve over all that has been lost, and those whose loyalty and ethics have been so compromised by their experience that they turn hostile, self-centered, and subversive. These "three armies" are found among the winners as well as the losers in corporate wars.

The problem of survivors is seldom on the minds of the planners of change, but it cannot be avoided by those who must implement the change or those who must manage the situation that results from it. When *Boardroom Reports* recently interviewed S. R. Heath, the executive vice president for administration at Manville Corporation, he discussed the problem of survivors. Manville's asbestos-related liabilities had forced a Chapter 11 bankruptcy filing and a workforce reduction of almost 40%. Heath was asked what surprised him the most about this painful process.

"I guess it was the problems of the survivors," he replied. "We didn't realize that the survivors would need as much help as those who were leaving. We were focusing most of our efforts on those departing. . . . We ultimately determined that professional help was needed to rebuild the teams and relationships that were disturbed by the layoffs."

Not all organizations have to face the prospect of such deep cuts, but Heath's comments must be heard by the leaders of organizations that are currently undertaking reorganizations or personnel cutbacks of significant scope. One of the ironies of today's organizational world is that the current

121

mania for trimming the organizational waistline is justified in the name of organizational health. Having made these cuts, organizations discover that the only remaining source of cost savings is greater and more efficient effort by their employees. But then they discover that those employees are the "survivors," whose energy has been sapped and whose commitment has been weakened by unmanaged or mismanaged transition.

Another of the ironies of the organizational world is that outplacement services have become an accepted way to assist terminated employees but that no comparable body of services has been developed to help those who are left behind. There are really two ironies. First, money and effort are being focused on the people who are no longer with the company. The survivors, on whose efforts and motivation the future of the company depends, get little or no attention. Second, the kinds of training offered terminated employees by an outplacement program are designed to equip them to find work and manage their careers in a continually changing business environment. These are the resourceful employees the company needs, but as a result of outplacement training, such employees are now working for the company's competitors.

I think of such matters whenever I read articles about the changes today's organizations are being urged to make to become competitive or profitable. *INC.* magazine recently ran such an article, listing 10 things manufacturing companies need to do to be successful today. Their "Ten Commandments for the New Manufacturing" are as follows:

> *The leavers have adjusted better than the stayers.*
>
> Exxon VP, describing the aftermath of the company's downsizing

"1. Keep production units small.

 2. Keep corporate overhead low.

 3. Keep productivity high.

 4. Keep production flexible.

 5. Remain market driven.

 6. Customize products.

 7. Strive for margins, not volume.

 8. Stress customer service.

 9. Recruit from the New America [i.e., outside the white, male, young mainstream].

10. Recruit a CEO with non-manufacturing experience."[1]

All of these things make good sense, but think of the transitions that any of them—much less all 10 at once—involve. Each of these changes will force people to let go of their old worlds, leave them in the neutral zone for an extended period, and then call on them to learn new behaviors and develop new attitudes. The *INC.* list and others like it are recommending transition times 10.

Today's organizations are reeling from the human impacts of the changes that have been forced on them by technology, international competition, and demographics. What is the prescription for this condition? More change. It is like taking the hair of the dog that bit you as a hangover remedy. And it is actually worse than that, for when Change 1 does not cure the hangover, the organization tries Change 2 and Change 3 in rapid succession.

We are still caught in the mid-twentieth-century mindset, which conceived of the main organizational problem as *the lack of change.* That outlook led to the idea of the change agent—a person who knew how to enter an organization, often from outside, and change things. But as we approach the end of the century, we're increasingly faced with the fact that *the current problem is change itself.* It's the problem of "survivors" of yesterday's change projects, and everyone is a survivor.

This is why transition management is such a critical skill for you to develop. You're going to find yourself dealing with the aftermath of mismanaged or unmanaged transition every time you turn around. That aftermath is a manager's nightmare. To remind myself of its characteristics, I use the acronym GRASS:

Guilt: Managers (including you) feel guilty that they have had to terminate, transfer, and demote people. Workers who survived when others were cut feel guilty too. Guilt lowers self-esteem and often leads to one of two kinds of overcompensation: permissiveness to make up for the earlier harsh acts, or an even harsher "blaming the victim," which projects the responsibility for the guilt away from the person who feels it.

Resentment: Everyone, manager and managed alike, feels angry at the organization for the pain that transition causes. This is natural. But when that aspect of the grieving process is not managed sensitively, the anger deepens and lengthens into a continuing resentment that poisons the whole organization. When yesterday's changes leave such a heritage of resentment, today's changes are undermined before they are launched.

The winners of tomorrow will deal proactively with chaos, will look at the chaos per se as the source of market advantage, not as a problem to be got around.

Tom Peters, American writer

In addition, resentment is the cause of sabotage and the subtler forms of resistance that organizations experience today.

Anxiety: People who are trying to hold onto the past while pieces of it are being cut away are anxious. The strange thing is that some managers believe that anxiety improves motivation. Perhaps a bit of anxiety does that, but in the quantity that is common in many organizations today, anxiety reduces energy, lowers motivation, and makes people unwilling to try new things.

Self-absorption: Anxious people become preoccupied with their own situations and lose their concern for fellow workers or customers. In a game of musical chairs, the only real questions are, "When is the music going to stop, and will there be a chair left for me?" Larger issues of teamwork, good service, and high quality get fuzzy when the focus is so nearsightedly personal as this. Nor do pep talks on the values of teamwork, good service, and high quality do much good when people are self-absorbed. They simply do not absorb inspiration well in that state.

Stress: I've already talked about the increase in the rate of illness and accident when people are in transition. Most organizations respond with stress management programs, which are certainly better than nothing but which do little to counter the sources of stress. Creating stress and then trying to "manage" it is like trying to cool your overheated brakes. The only real answer is to take your foot off the brake.

How poor are they who have not patience! What wound did ever heal but by degrees?
William Shakespeare

GRASS: Guilt, Resentment, Anxiety, Self-Absorption, and Stress. These are the five real and measurable costs of not managing transition effectively. Remember them the next time people tell you there isn't time to worry about the reactions of your employees to the latest plan for change. And help such people to see that the failure to manage transition is really a shortcut that costs much more than it saves. For it leaves behind a fatigued and demoralized workforce at the very time when everyone agrees that the only way American organizations can be successful is to get more out of their employees.

The other thing to remember and help others to understand is that there are well-tested, effective ways to avoid these difficulties. Many organizations follow the path toward their own collapse simply because people do not know there is another way.

This is all the more important because if we know anything about the future, it is that it will be different from the present. Whatever is, will change.

What it will look like is something that the futurists can debate. The only certainty is that between *here* and *there* will be a lot of change. Where there's change, there's transition. That's the utterly predictable equation:

$$\text{change} + \text{human beings} = \text{transition.}$$

There's no way to avoid it. But you can manage it. *You* can. And if you want to come through in one piece, you *must*.

Our moral responsibility is not to stop the future, but to shape it . . . to channel our destiny in humane directions and to ease the trauma of transition.

Alvin Toffler, American futurist

---

[1] "Ten Commandments of Manufacturing," *INC.,* November 1990, 21.

Index

About the Author

William Bridges is a preeminent authority on change and managing change in the workplace. A former literature professor, he was trained at Harvard, Columbia, and Brown, where he received his Ph.D. in American Civilization in 1963. He initiated his own career change to become a counselor and consultant, founding William Bridges & Associates in 1981 to help organizations and individuals deal more successfully with transition.

William Bridges's training programs, speeches, and consulting have been utilized by several hundred organizations, including Pacific Bell, Baxter Healthcare, Intel, Apple Computer, Kaiser Permanente, Proctor & Gamble, Hewlett-Packard, the U.S. Forest Service, Chevron Corporation, Kal Kan Foods, and McDonnell Douglas Astronautics. *The Wall Street Journal* has listed him among the top ten independent executive development presenters in the U.S. For more information on his publications and services, contact:

William Bridges & Associates
38 Miller Avenue, Suite 12
Mill Valley, CA 94941
Telephone: (415) 381-9663
Fax: (415) 381-8124
Internet: wmbridges@wmbridges.com

More Books on Understanding Transition by William Bridges

Transitions
Making Sense of Life's Changes

With more than 250,000 copies sold, this classic shows how making a successful transition through difficult times lets you recognize and seize opportunities. Learn to recognize the three stages of any transition: Endings, the Neutral Zone, and the New Beginning.

$13.00, paperback, 170 pages
ISBN 0-201-00082-2

Jobshift
How to Prosper in a Workplace without Jobs

"The first 53 pages alone provide the most cogent, up-to-date account I've seen of what's happening to traditional notions of work, jobs, and careers—and why; and what it means for current and future generations of Americans." —*Inc.*

$13.00, paperback, 257 pages
ISBN 0-201-48933-5

To order, please contact:

Corporate, Government, and Special Sales
Addison-Wesley Publishing Company
One Jacob Way
Reading, MA   01867-3999
(800)822-6339